THE ILLUSTRATED HISTORY OF THE WORLD

Rome and the Ancient World

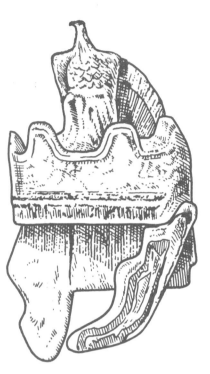

PREFACE

The Illustrated History of the World is a unique series of eight volumes covering the entire scope of human history, from the days of the nomadic hunters up to the present. Each volume surveys significant events and personages, key political and economic developments, and the critical forces that inspired change, in both institutions and the everyday life of people around the globe.

The books are organized on a spread-by-spread basis, allowing ease of access and depth of coverage on a wide range of fascinating topics and time periods within any one volume. Each spread serves as a kind of mini-essay, in words and pictures, of its subject. The text—cogent, concise and lively—is supplemented by an impressive array of illustrations (original art, full-color photographs, maps, diagrams) and features (glossary, index, time charts, further reading listings). Taking into account the new emphasis on multicultural education, special care has been given to presenting a balanced portrait of world history: the volumes in the series explore all civilizations—whether it's the Mayans in Mexico, the Shoguns in Japan or the Sumerians in the Middle East.

Rome and the Ancient World

Mike Corbishley

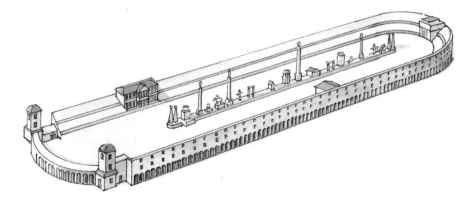

Facts On File

Text copyright © 1993 by Mike Corbishley
Illustrations copyright © 1993 by Simon & Schuster Young Books
All rights reserved. No part of this book may be reproduced or utilized
in any form or by any means, electronic or mechanical, including
photocopying, recording, or by any information storage or retrieval
systems, without permission in writing from the publisher. For
information contact:
Facts On File, Inc.
460 Park Avenue South
New York NY 10016

Corbishley, Mike.
Rome and the ancient world/Mike Corbishley.
p.   cm.
Includes bibliographical references and index.
Summary: Explores the history of the Roman Empire and the world
outside the Empire, including ancient China, ancient India, and the
empires of Africa.
ISBN 0-8160-2786-2
1. Rome—History—Juvenile literature. 2. History, Ancient—
Juvenile literature. [2. Rome—History. 2. History, Ancient.]
I. Title.
DG209.C69   1993
930—dc20
91-43789
CIP
AC

ISBN 0 8160 2786 2

Facts On File books are available at special discounts when purchased
in bulk quantities for businesses, associations, institutions or sales
promotions. Please call our Special Sales Department in New York at
212/683-2244 (dial 800/322-8755 except in NY, AK or HI).

Designed by Hammond Hammond
Composition by Goodfellow and Egan Ltd, Cambridge
Printed and Bound by BPCC Hazell Books, Paulton and Aylesbury

10 9 8 7 6 5 4 3 2 1

This book is printed on acid-free paper.

First Published in Great Britain in 1991 by
Simon and Schuster Young Books

CONTENTS

INTRODUCTION

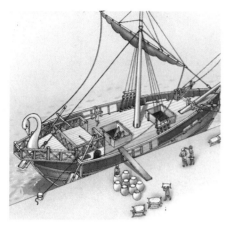

What sort of place was the Ancient World? Who lived in it? And when did they live? These questions are not as easy to answer as they seem. An English novelist once wrote "The past is a foreign country; they do things differently there." In other words, it is sometimes difficult for us today to understand what really happened in the past. The best we can do is to find glimpses of what happened when we read what was written at the time and when we visit remains of things which still exist.

Throughout this book you will be shown evidence for the peoples and places of the past. Archaeologists and historians do not always know exactly what the evidence means. Sometimes we have to make a guess.

In Part One of this book you will read about the world of the Romans. The Romans introduced their way of life to millions of people over a huge area around the Mediterranean Sea. They were famous in their own times for their military discipline, their organization and their buildings and construction of things such as roads. Some of the peoples who had lived a simple life as farmers for hundreds of years were suddenly able to see great stone buildings, running water and plays at the theater. The Romans also brought these people slavery, butchery of human beings and animals for 'sport,' and the end of their own way of life. Other nations, like the Greeks, had already developed an advanced civilization of their own long before Roman times.

The Romans had an enormous influence on later peoples in Europe. The Roman way of life and government went on into the Middle Ages in the Eastern Mediterranean. Their language, Latin, can still be seen in many European languages today.

In Part Two you will travel beyond the borders of the Roman Empire to look at a whole variety of different peoples—from Africa to India and even to China. But they all have one thing in common. They were either conquered by Rome or at least traded with Rome. Some peoples, like those in China, provided rich goods for trade but remained untouched by Roman invasions. Others were not as lucky. As you will see, nations such as the Parthians, for example, were conquered in the end.

ATLANTIC
OCEAN

• LONDINIUM

The eagle was the symbol
of the Roman Empire.

BLACK
SEA

• MASSILIA

• ROME

• BYZANTIUM

• ATHENS

• CARTHAGE

MEDITERRANEAN
SEA

**The Roman Empire
in AD 200**

• ALEXANDRIA

— Outlines of provinces

PART ONE

The Roman World

The map on this page shows the world known to the Romans in the second century AD. They created a huge empire. A small group of people in Italy were able to become a world power. You can see the area they *conquered* with their armies, but beyond that, in all directions, were lands and peoples the Romans traded with. For example, they imported silks from as far away as China.

The world of the Romans was not only big, it also lasted a very long time. Although it is difficult to say exactly when Rome began to develop, the Romans themselves used to teach their children that the city was founded in 753 BC. It was over a thousand years later that the Roman Empire came to an end.

FROM ALL OVER THE EMPIRE In AD 80 the Roman poet Martial wrote about people from all over the Empire coming to the opening of Rome's greatest amphitheater, the Colosseum:

There are farmers from the Balkans here, natives from southern Russia bred on horses' blood, people who drink the Nile's waters and even those from far away Britain. Arabs, people from the shores of the Red Sea, as well as those from southern Turkey, have hurried here and German tribesmen and Ethiopians each with their own peculiar hairstyles.

THE IDEA OF BEING ROMAN Martial himself lived for over 30 years in Rome, the capital city of the Empire. But he grew up in Bilbilis in Spain, a new town created by the Romans in one of their *provinces*.

One of the important things which helps make people feel they belong to an empire is a single language. The language of the Roman Empire was Latin. The 60 million people living in the Roman Empire did not all speak Latin as their first language. But Latin was the *official* language and if you wanted to do well you had to master it.

EVIDENCE FOR THE ROMAN PAST How do we know about the Romans and their world? Writing and literature give us part of the *evidence*. The other important sources of evidence are the things that remain. Many Roman buildings can still be seen above ground, and archaeologists have excavated many others, as well as the thousands of Roman objects you can see today in museums. If you live in or visit countries that were once part of the Roman world, you are never far away from the Romans themselves! Read on.

THE FOUNDING OF ROME

To understand the early history of the Romans we must first look back to a people known as the Etruscans. They lived in an area north of Rome, called Etruria, which was hilly but fertile. By the seventh century BC, these Etruscans had formed themselves into 12 independent states. Each state had its own capital city, but the people all thought of themselves as Etruscans. Together they began to conquer lands beyond Etruria and by the sixth century BC there were Etruscan cities from Salerno in the south to Mantua in the north.

This is an antefix which decorated the ridge line of a building in the Etruscan town of Veii and dates from the sixth century BC. It is made of clay and fired in a kiln and was once even more highly painted.

THE SKILFUL ETRUSCANS The Etruscans were farmers who grew grain, olives and grapes. They also made money by trade (selling their extra corn, for example) with peoples such as the Greeks. They were skilled metalworkers and potters. Their cities were properly planned out with streets, *aqueducts* (for bringing water) and sewage systems.

We know quite a lot about the Etruscans from the beautifully decorated tombs which have been discovered. The Etruscans believed in a life after death and the rich built underground tombs for their dead. They buried them with objects such as vases, statues and jewellery. The walls of the tombs were painted with scenes of Etruscan life.

OTHER TRIBES The Etruscans were not the only people in this part of Italy at this time, although they were the most powerful. Other tribes were called the Samnites, the Umbrians, the Sabines and the Latins. The Latins were the biggest of the tribes and had arrived in this area, probably from across the Alps, before the eighth century BC. Their name, of course, shows that they spoke the Latin language.

THE CITY OF ROME The Latins lived around and in the city of Rome – 'Roma' was originally an Etruscan word. The early history of the city of Rome reveals the complicated history of Italy at this time. Rome was governed first by a Sabine, then a Latin, another Sabine and then three Etruscan kings. The Romans themselves believed that their first ruler or king (*rex*) was Romulus who had founded the city of Rome on 21 April 753 BC. Perhaps you have read the story of the twins, Romulus and Remus, who were left to die as babies in a basket floating on the River Tiber. The story tells how they were brought up by a she-wolf. Romulus killed his brother Remus in an argument.

This bronze statue of the wolf which suckled Romulus and Remus was made by an Etruscan craftsman in the sixth century BC. The twins were added in the sixteenth century AD.

The city of Rome was originally separate villages built on seven hills overlooking the River Tiber. They were the Quirinal, Viminal, Esquiline, Caelian, Aventine, Palatine and Capitoline hills. The Etruscans combined the villages into the first proper town of Roma. The valleys in between the hills began to be occupied with houses, shops and businesses. The River Tiber connected the growing town with the sea which meant easy trade with the rest of Italy and abroad. Later a port called Ostia was established at the mouth of the River Tiber.

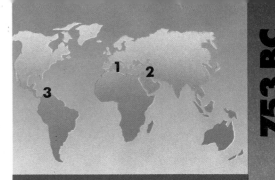

Italy in 241 BC

The Romans gradually increased their control over Italy with the help of their allies. Colonies were set up by Roman citizens. The dates of these colonies are given on the map. Other peoples were made Roman either by giving them full or half citizenship.

1 From about 1500 BC to 100 BC (when the Etruscans first appeared in Italy) there were a number of small kingdoms on mainland Greece and on other islands. There were royal palaces at Mycenae, in the Peloponnese south of Athens, and at Knossos on Crete. By about 1450 BC the Mycenaeans had taken over the civilization on Crete. The cities in mainland Greece became important. In the fifth century BC they were threatened by the Persian Empire. At a famous battle in the Bay of Marathon the Persians were defeated in 490 BC, and again at Salamis in 480 BC.

2 The Phoenicians were descendants of the Canaanites (from Israel) and were known throughout the ancient world as sea traders. From the ninth century BC onwards they established colonies in the southern Mediterranean. The most famous is at Carthage in north Africa.

3 Between 1200 BC and 300 BC the villages in parts of central America became the centers of complex civilizations. One of the most famous were the Olmec people known for their art carved in stone. They occupied a relatively small area on the southern shores of the Gulf of Mexico between 1200 BC and 300 BC.

ARIMINUM 268

ADRIATIC SEA

SPOLETIUM 241

COSA 273

ROME

TYRRHENIAN SEA

AESERNIA 263

BENEVENTUM 268

BRUNDISIUM 244

PAESTUM 273

Roman territory (full citizenship)

Roman territory (half citizenship)

Roman colony

Romanized peoples

Allies of Rome

Date of colony   268

The Etruscans liked highly decorated objects. On the left is a vase of fired clay of a type known as bucchero which was grey all the way through. On the right is a little gold pot from the tomb of a wealthy Etruscan buried in Praeneste. It dates from the seventh century BC.

11

THE ROMAN REPUBLIC

The forum in Rome seen from the Capitoline Hill was the center of political life. In the background is the Colosseum.

The Latin-speaking people of the city of Rome had been governed by rulers from other tribes in the earliest part of their history. The first kings had divided the population of Rome into different tribes. A king had a group of men to advise him. Later, people were allowed to vote on important matters in an assembly. They had rights according to how rich they were.

ETRUSCAN KINGS The third of the Etruscan kings of Rome, called Lucius Tarquinius, was nicknamed 'the Proud'. He was hated for his harsh rule and was thrown out by the Roman people. A much later ruler of Rome, the Emperor Claudius, wrote:

Then, after what King Tarquinius the Proud did, he came to be hated by the people of Rome. We were all thoroughly fed up with being ruled by kings and the government was put in the hands of officials who were elected each year.

THE REPUBLIC OF ROME Roman historians tell us that the date a completely new form of government was created was 509 BC. It was called *res publica* which literally meant 'a matter for the people.' From it comes our word republic. A republic is a form of government where all the officials who govern are voted into office by the citizens. This is what happened in Rome.

ELECTED OFFICIALS The Romans hated the word 'king' and so their first act was to make it impossible for one person to have complete power – even if that person was voted into office. So they created two officials called *consuls*. They had much the same power as kings and were in charge of the government and the army. But

they were only in office for one year and had to agree on policies with each other.

To cope with a serious emergency, the consuls could appoint a *dictator* who held absolute power for a period of six months. It was especially useful in war to have just one supreme commander. The dictator had a second-in-command called a *magister equitum* (it means 'master of the horse') who was in charge of the *cavalry*.

THE ROMAN SENATE In normal circumstances a parliament, called the *senate*, made up of ex-officials, helped the consuls to reach decisions, and discussed all the important issues of the day.

There were four other chief officials of the government. *Praetors* were the chief judges of the Roman Republic elected each year. They were the most important officials of government after the consuls. Every five years *censors* were elected, originally to take a *census*, or count, of the citizens. The two censors held office for eighteen months. They registered all citizens and their properties and put them into tribes and classes for voting and military service. *Quaestors* were first appointed by the consuls as assistants to help as magistrates in the courts of law. Later four quaestors were elected and two of them looked after the state's finances. *Aediles* were four officials who were in charge of all public works and public records. For example, they were responsible for ensuring a proper water supply to the city through aqueducts.

PATRICIANS, PLEBEIANS AND EQUITES The people of Rome were divided into classes – at first there were two and then a third was added. The wealthy people who owned land were called *patricians*. They could trace their origins back to the noble families of early Rome. The patricians could vote and could assume government positions, such as consul. All the ordinary people were known as *plebeians*. They could vote but could only hold minor posts in the government. The plebeians were able to elect ten officials, called *tribunes*, each year who looked after their interests in the government.

The third class of people in Rome was created later from the growing number of business men who owned property. They were called the *equites* ('knights').

Not every adult person in the Roman Republic could vote. Women and slaves were excluded.

Plebeians formed the largest class in Roman society – workers who usually owned no property. They organized themselves, made protests and won the right to hold some political offices by 287 BC.

Patricians were the aristocracy of Rome – the privileged class. They held all the most important political and religious offices.

Equites was the name for the second rank of Roman nobles who were rich enough to provide a horse and equipment for the cavalry. The Emperor Augustus allowed any free man of blameless character to become a 'knight' on payment of 400,000 sesterces.

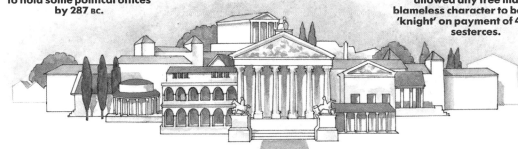

The Government of Rome

Praetors were the highest level of magistrates in Roman courts of law.

Normally in wars the two consuls would take charge of the army.

The Senate was the place where the affairs of state were discussed – similar to a modern parliament.

Consuls held the supreme power of both the civilian government and the army. During the Republican period the consuls were voted in by the assembly of the people. But they had to be proposed by senators from their own ranks. They retained power for a year (beginning on January 1) until the period of the emperors when they remained in office for two to four months only.

An aedile's job involved the care for the city's water supply.

Censors were first appointed in about 443 BC to compile the census of the male property-owning population.

Aediles had the job of looking after public buildings and the state archives.

Tarquin the Proud

According to tradition and Roman sources the last three kings of Rome were all Etruscan. Many stories were told about the early years of Rome – not all can possibly be true. One, which was a favorite for Roman children, was about the last king of all – Lucius Tarquinius – who murdered the former king, Tullius. He acted as cruel dictator from the start of his reign. He took rights away from the people and put to death the patricians whose land or wealth he wanted for himself. He was nicknamed 'Superbus' (the Proud) by the Roman people who hated him. He increased the power of Rome by defeating neighboring tribes, including the Volscians. After 24 years of this tyrant's rule the people banished him in 510 BC. He fled to the Etruscan town of Caere. He led various uprisings against Rome but eventually died at Cumae.

THE ARMY IN THE REPUBLIC

Rome had always needed an army to protect its own citizens from other tribes. The Romans also wanted to conquer lands around the city, and later further afield. When the Romans were ruled by kings, each of the three Roman tribes provided 1000 men for an infantry regiment and 100 men with horses for a cavalry squadron. The size of the army increased as the state became bigger. But during the Republic it was not a permanent army but was called together in times of trouble.

THE CALL-UP The heads of state, the consuls, appointed officers, called *tribuni militum* ('military tribunes'). It was the tribunes' job to recruit the right number of men for the regiment, or *legio* ('legion') as it was called. Any free citizen who owned property had to assemble in Rome and could be chosen by the tribunes to join the army for a particular campaign.

WEAPONS AND WARFARE The infantry soldiers of the legions – legionnaries – were put into different fighting units according to their age and physical strength. The front line troops were fully armed and carried two javelins to hurl against the enemy. Behind them came the older men, used in emergencies in the battle. They each carried a long spear. The last group were the skirmishers. These were the poorest citizens who could only afford to equip themselves with light armor and carry short javelins.

OFFICERS AND CAVALRY Each part of each legion had a number of officers to command the men and control the battle. A cavalry squadron was formed from the wealthiest citizens – those who could afford the horse, weapons and armor. Because the Roman citizens could never afford enough cavalry, the allies of Rome provided the largest number of mounted soldiers in the army as well as an equal number of infantrymen.

ON CAMPAIGN On the march, the soldiers of the allies marched first, followed by the rest of the army. They went in battle order if they were in hostile territory. At the end of each day, one of the tribunes chose a suitable site for the camp. To make the camp, the legionnaries

Roman

Roman allies

Latin

Rebels

Italy During the War with the Allies

The Romans initially refused to make their allies in Italy full citizens of the Roman state. In 91 BC a revolt broke out, which finally came to an end in 89 BC.

ROME

POMPEII

BRUNDISIUM

THURII

The eagle, the symbol of the king of the gods – Jupiter – was adopted by the Romans as their symbol of authority and power. It appeared on coins, in sculpture and on the standards carried in battle. Here it tops a helmet of a centurion in the Roman army. Centurions were in charge of 100-man units and had to be tough soldiers. To survive campaigns to reach this rank they had to be very experienced.

Lined up for battle the Roman army was a formidable sight for their enemies. On the left you can see the three types of foot soldiers. The *triarius* (standing left) were so called because, as experienced soldiers, they formed the rear rank in battle. The two front lines were formed by the *hastatus* or *princeps* (kneeling), less experienced but still young enough to fight. The *velites* (standing right) were lightly armed with helmets (this one has a wolf skin over it) and spears. They were used as skirmishers. In front of the troops (below) you can see a horn blower who gave out orders from the commanders. On the right is a standard bearer. There was one standard bearer for each legion, and one for each *centuria* (a century = 100 men). This is one of the century standard bearers.

The Organization of the Army

CAVALRY										
										TRIARII
										PRINCIPES
										HASTATI

Two centuries made up one *manipulus*. Within each century were the following officers and soldiers:

Centurion unit commander
Optio second-in-command
Cornicen trumpeteer
Signifer standard bearer

The organization of the soldiers in a legion, headed by six tribunes.

Tesserarius guard commander
Hastati foot soldiers
Principes foot soldiers
Velites foot soldiers/skirmishers
    A legion was made up of 10 *manipuli* of the following types of soldiers:
Hastati front line foot soldiers
Principes second line foot soldiers
Triarii rear line foot soldiers
10 squadrons of cavalry
    The legion was commanded by six tribunes.

dug a deep ditch and formed a bank, called the *rampart*, to protect the army. On top of the rampart a strong wooden fence was made of stakes. Each soldier carried two stakes. Everyone knew exactly where to pitch their tents inside the camp because it was always laid out in the same way.

INTO BATTLE The Romans were careful to adopt tried-and-tested battle procedures that they could use again and again. Normally the consuls would set out their army in this way: in the center of the battle line were the legions. On each side were the legions of the allies and on the wings were the cavalry squadrons. At the start of the battle the light-armed troops and cavalry would try to unnerve the enemy by fast attacks in small groups. Then in the center the main army would advance, first hurling their spears and then fighting at close quarters. Each legionary carried a short sword and a dagger as well as a long shield. The army commanders made sure that their men were trained in formation fighting, and that they were disciplined and obeyed orders in battle.

ENEMIES OF ROME: GAULS, SAMNITES AND GREEKS

The Gauls and the Geese

When the Gauls, who were fierce warriors, reached Rome and beseiged the city the people fled and took refuge on one of the high points of the city called the Capitoline Hill. The Gauls crept up on the sleeping Romans at night but, as the Roman historian, Livy, tells us:

One by one the Gauls pulled themselves up the side of the hill and reached the top. They were so silent that not even the guard dogs were woken up . . . but the Gauls could not escape the notice of the geese, which were sacred to the goddess Juno. These geese saved the Romans by their cackling and the flapping of their wings.

The Latin people of Rome needed a large army in order to remain the most powerful tribe in their area. In the area closest to the city of Rome there were three tribes they had to conquer. The Sabines lived to the north-east. The Aequi lived in the mountainous areas in central Italy. The Volsci lived close to Rome itself. The Romans had conquered all these peoples by 304 BC.

The Etruscans were still powerful in Italy and the Romans had to deal with them, too. They proved difficult to conquer but were eventually defeated.

THE GAULS Celtic tribes called the Gauls came across the Alps in about 400 BC to look for new land in Italy. One Roman historian, Polybius, said that they, *spent their time in war or farming and that their only possessions were cattle and gold because this is what they could carry about with them.*

In 390 BC the Gauls became a real threat to the city of Rome itself. They besieged the city and would have broken in by night if they had not been spotted in time. Eventually the Romans were forced to pay them a very large sum of gold to leave the country.

THE SAMNITES A greater threat to the Romans than the Gauls were the Samnites who lived in villages in central Italy south of Rome. Originally the Romans had signed a treaty with the Samnites to help them both conquer the Volsci. But they were both powerful peoples and only one could take overall control. War broke out in 343 BC and lasted for 50 years. Samnite warriors were difficult to

This sculpture comes from the tomb of Mausolus, the Greek ruler of Caria in Asia. It shows the story of the Greeks fighting the Amazons. You can see that the Greeks wore little armor except for their distinctive helmets and round shields.

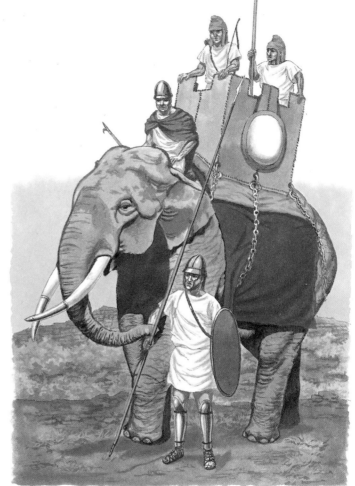

Left. Samnite warriors carried a shield called a scutum to protect their bodies and armor which included a breast plate, greaves (leg armor), a wide sword belt and a helmet with cheek pieces. They carried long spears like the Romans. Their horsemen were not as well protected.

Above. A captured Gaul is shown chained to a tree which is hung with weapons collected from battle. It is part of an arch built at Carpentras, in the south of France, to celebrate the defeat of the Celtic peoples in Gaul by the Romans.

Right. Typical Greek soldiers. 'The greatest defeat of the day was caused by the unstoppable force of the elephants of King Pyrrhus' wrote the historian Plutarch. Elephants were trained to charge the enemy and sometimes carried an armored box for soldiers as here.

fight against because they were very heavily armed. The Romans copied the Samnite idea of a long rectangular shield. The Romans suffered several defeats in their wars against the Samnites but eventually conquered them in 290 BC when the Samnites agreed to become allies of Rome.

THE GREEKS Throughout the fourth and third centuries BC the Romans established their superior position in Italy by a combination of conquest, alliances with other tribes and by establishing *colonies*, or new towns. The people of these new colonies had a territory to control around it and this was a good way of introducing the Roman way of life to that area.

Other peoples had also set up colonies. In the south of Italy the Greeks had established a new Greek land called *Magna Graecia* (Great Greece) which contained many Greek colonies. The Romans wanted to force these Greek colonies to join them. The colonies objected and asked the Greek king of Epirus, Pyrrhus, for help. In 280 BC he came with a huge force – 25,000 soldiers and 20 war elephants. Pyrrhus also enlisted the help of enemies of Rome in southern Italy. The Romans raised about the same number of troops and although they lost 7,000 men in the first battle with Pyrrhus they eventually won. In 275 BC Pyrrhus returned to Greece with only about two-thirds of his army.

The Romans were now in control of all of Italy. But they were about to face their biggest threat – the Carthaginians.

ENEMIES OF ROME: HANNIBAL AND THE CARTHAGINIANS

A sea-trading people called the Phoenicians established the city of Carthage in north Africa. Its people, the Carthaginians, had established their control over the large area of the Mediterranean, including the island of Sicily.

THE FIRST WAR The first war with Carthage lasted 23 years and began in 264 BC. It started when the Carthaginians moved out of the territory they held in the south-west of Sicily and occupied the town of Messana (now modern Messina). This was the closest town to the mainland of Italy. The Romans sent two legions and beat their enemy.

But the Romans did not defeat the Carthaginians easily or quickly. The Romans were not good at fighting at sea and had to build two huge fleets to overcome the Carthaginian navy. When the war was over the Romans forced them to pay a huge fine in silver.

HANNIBAL – CARTHAGINIAN COMMANDER-IN-CHIEF After this first war with Rome, the Carthaginian commander, Hamilcar Barca, led his forces into Spain in 237 BC to defend the settlements established there and win some more territory. It was here that his son, Hannibal, became commander-in-chief of the Carthaginian forces at the age of 25.

The Romans considered these new campaigns in Spain and southern Gaul (now southern France) a threat to them, especially when Hannibal besieged the town of Saguntum on the northeast coast. The Romans had made a treaty with Saguntum and sent two armies against Hannibal. One went to Africa from southern Italy, the other to Massilia (now Marseilles) to confront Hannibal's army.

HANNIBAL CROSSES THE ALPS Unfortunately for the Romans, Hannibal left southern Gaul before they arrived and began an incredible journey across the Alps to reach Italy and the heart of the Romans' territory. Hannibal's army had about 40,000 men in it as well as 37 war elephants. The journey was so difficult that by the time it finally reached Italy the army had been reduced to about 26,000 men and 12 elephants.

At first Hannibal was successful against the Romans

Hannibal lost an enormous number of men and animals, crossing the Alps into the heart of Roman territory.

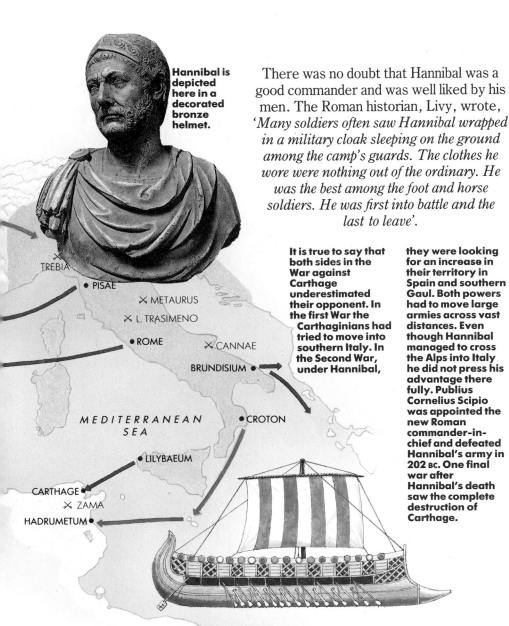

Hannibal is depicted here in a decorated bronze helmet.

There was no doubt that Hannibal was a good commander and was well liked by his men. The Roman historian, Livy, wrote, *'Many soldiers often saw Hannibal wrapped in a military cloak sleeping on the ground among the camp's guards. The clothes he wore were nothing out of the ordinary. He was the best among the foot and horse soldiers. He was first into battle and the last to leave'.*

It is true to say that both sides in the War against Carthage underestimated their opponent. In the first War the Carthaginians had tried to move into southern Italy. In the Second War, under Hannibal, they were looking for an increase in their territory in Spain and southern Gaul. Both powers had to move large armies across vast distances. Even though Hannibal managed to cross the Alps into Italy he did not press his advantage there fully. Publius Cornelius Scipio was appointed the new Roman commander-in-chief and defeated Hannibal's army in 202 BC. One final war after Hannibal's death saw the complete destruction of Carthage.

1 The earliest towns and cities in southeast Asia are in Vietnam where the fortified town of Co Loa is dated to the third century BC. The civilization developed here from complex societies living in village settlements but producing fine quality metal and fired clay goods. Towns like Co Loa were not densely occupied with houses but served as religious and trading centers for large areas around. The fortifications are in the form of stone walls and sometimes moats.

2 The Maya were a people who occupied the Yucatan peninsula in Central America creating their wealth from maize which they regarded as the greatest gift of the gods. By 300 BC they were building great ceremonial centers for their religion and their administration. These centers developed into full-scale cities by AD 300. The city of Tikal, for example, had a population of 50,000 at this time. The Maya built stepped pyramids with temples on the top where they carried out elaborate ceremonies. They believed that certain days were controlled by particular gods and chose the time carefully to carry out their activities. They developed writing, astronomy and mathematics. Their numbering system had units of 20 and they calculated their dates from a time (in our calendar system) in August 3114 BC.

3 At this time in Britain, society was well developed with the country divided between a number of tribes whose names we know from Roman literature. Some people lived in centers which were well fortified with walls, banks of earth and ditches. Some of these were hilltop settlements, now called hillforts. One of the largest, and most famous is Maiden Castle in Dorset where the local people resisted the Romans after their invasion in AD 43. Art was well developed and skilled craftspeople made pottery, jewelry and weapons.

TREBIA
PISAE
× METAURUS
× L. TRASIMENO
ROME
× CANNAE
BRUNDISIUM
MEDITERRANEAN SEA
CROTON
LILYBAEUM
CARTHAGE
× ZAMA
HADRUMETUM

and defeated them in several major battles. Eventually the Romans won a battle in Italy and then attacked Carthage itself. Carthage was taken in 146 BC and its inhabitants, 50,000 in all, were made slaves. Carthage and the territory it had once held became the new Roman province of Africa.

The Carthaginian Wars

☐	Under Carthagian control, 218 BC
▦	Under Roman control, 218 BC
→	Carthagian army
→	Roman army
×	Major battle

Key Dates in the Carthaginian Wars

First War
264 BC	Carthaginians occupy Messana in Sicily
260	Full-scale war
241	Carthage surrenders

Second War
221	Hannibal made Carthaginian commander
219	Saguntum captured. Romans declare war
218	The march across the Alps. Roman defeats
204	Romans invade north Africa
202	Carthaginian army defeated at Zama
183	Hannibal commits suicide

Third War
149	War breaks out
146	City of Carthage completely destroyed

THE END OF THE ROMAN REPUBLIC

The final defeat of the Carthaginians did not bring peace for the Romans. They had chosen to control people in Italy as well as to conquer new territories in many other parts of the Mediterranean.

After the wars with Carthage, there were other threats to Rome's new territories. The Cimbri, Teutones and Ambrones, tribes from northwestern Europe, invaded northern Italy and Gaul. King Mithradates VI, who ruled the lands south of the Black Sea, was defeated by the Romans in 63 BC. Pirates threatened Roman trade in the eastern Mediterranean. Nearer to home the Romans had to cope with uprisings of slaves and revolts of allies in Italy.

By 100 BC they controlled many of the lands surrounding the Mediterranean, including Spain, southern Gaul, Corsica, Sardinia, Carthage, Sicily, Greece and Asia (what is now Turkey). The Romans called these new territories *provinces* and each was governed by either an ex-consul (if the territory was important from a military point of view) or an ex-praetor.

It was during this time that the greatest strain was put on the republican form of government. In the senate house and in other public buildings (this is a basilica or public hall) politicians argued with each other or formed factions. Power had been held by such a few powerful families for so long. Tribunes of the people, like Tiberius and Gaius Gracchus, fought to give poorer people both land and some political rights.

THE NEED FOR LAND During these campaigns to acquire new territories the Roman state took control of a huge amount of farming land. This was normally given or let to farmers who were already rich. Poor smallholders often had land taken away from them and free farm workers were replaced by slave labour. There was a need for changes in the law to protect the poorer people. A tribune, Tiberius Gracchus, proposed a law which allowed this newly-acquired land to be given to poor farmers. Wealthy Romans in positions of power in the government opposed this law and had Tiberius murdered. His brother Gaius took up the reform but he too was murdered.

POLITICS IN ROME Apart from his strong views about land reform, Gaius was murdered because he wanted to reform the government and take some power away from one of the powerful groups in Rome – the senate. At this time in Rome there were two political parties. The Roman lawyer and politician Cicero explains the situation.

'In the Roman state there have always been two groups of people eager to take part in, and be leaders of, public life. One group wished to be known as the populares, the other as the optimates.'

You can almost work out what these two groups stood for from their names. The *optimates* (the word 'optimum' means best) were a group of very wealthy men who wanted to keep their wealth and their power. They tried to make sure that their chosen candidates were voted in to important positions. They particularly opposed the senate. The *populares* (think about the words 'popular' and 'population') were those who wanted reforms for ordinary working people and who wanted to take power away from the patricians and the senate.

CIVIL WARS This rivalry lead to clashes, street gangs, murders and eventually civil wars in the first century BC. Gaius Marius, for example, tried to win support for himself from the senate and ordinary people and marched on Rome with his army. He appointed himself consul seven times – completely illegal acts. He was opposed by Lucius Sulla who landed in Italy with a loyal army of 40,000 soldiers in 83 BC and began a civil war against Marius.

The whole idea of the Roman Republic with its officials voted in each year was beginning to fall apart as powerful politicians, backed by huge armies, took power for themselves as dictators. The second civil war was fought between Gnaeus Pompeius, better known by the name he gave himself – Magnus 'Pompey the Great' – and Julius Caesar. Pompey fought for the senate but his army, finally led by his son, was defeated in 45 BC.

The system of rule by kings, which the early Romans had been so against, had almost returned in the rule of

Key People and Dates in the Civil Wars

Cicero 106–43 BC (left). Marcus Tullius Cicero was the most well known of Roman public speakers. Originally a lawyer, he moved into politics. He sided with Pompey in the Civil War against Julius Caesar and was eventually put to death by Octavian who later became the Emperor Augustus.

Pompey 106–48 BC (below). Gnaeus Pompeius, now known as Pompey, fought with Sulla in the Civil War against Marius.

Sulla 138–78 BC (above). Lucius Cornelius Sulla brought about the Civil War in 83 BC by marching on Rome. He declared himself dictator and threw out the elected government who had declared him a 'public enemy'.

Marius 157–86 BC (above). Gaius Marius was elected consul many times. He defeated the Cimbri, the Teutones and the Ambrones.

123–122	Gaius Gracchus voted tribune
105	Romans defeated by Cimbri and Teutones
104–100	Consulships of Marius
102	Teutones defeated
101	Cimbri defeated
87	Revolt of Marius in Rome
82–81	Sulla created dictator
70	Consulship of Pompey and Crassus
63	Consulship of Cicero
60	Coalition of Pompey, Caesar and Crassus
59	Caesar voted consul
49–46	War between Caesar and his opponents
48	Death of Pompey
44	Assassination of Julius Caesar

dictators. Julius Caesar finally declared himself 'dictator for life' in 44 BC. He was murdered the same year. This did not stop the breakdown of the republican system. After more civil war the system finally changed and the Romans got a king again – although this time he was careful to call himself by a different name, Emperor of Rome.

The Roman Empire
INCREASING THE LIMITS OF THE EMPIRE

Julius Caesar became a consul in 59 BC. After he had held the highest position in the government of Rome he went to be governor of the provinces in northern Italy and Gaul. Caesar was a professional soldier and decided to invade the territories of the Celtic peoples in Gaul, Germany and Britain. By 54 BC he had established the northern boundary of the Roman world at what is now called the English Channel.

The politician Cicero spoke about Caesar in the senate:

Before, members of the senate, we had only a route through Gaul. All the

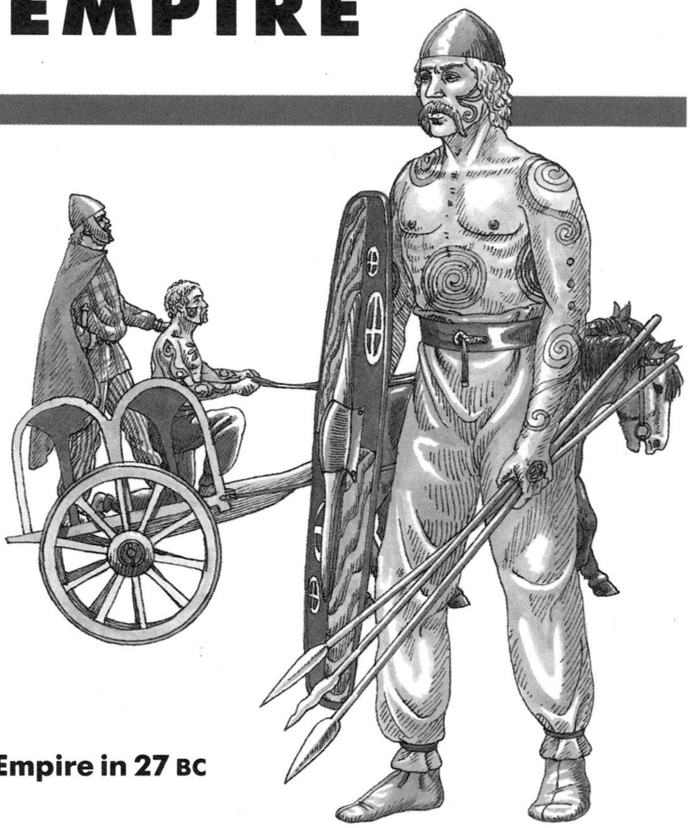

The Celtic peoples in Britain, tattooed and with wild war cries, fiercely resisted Caesar's invasions. 'Their usual method of fighting,' wrote Caesar, 'was from chariots dashing about all over the battlefield hurling their javelins.'

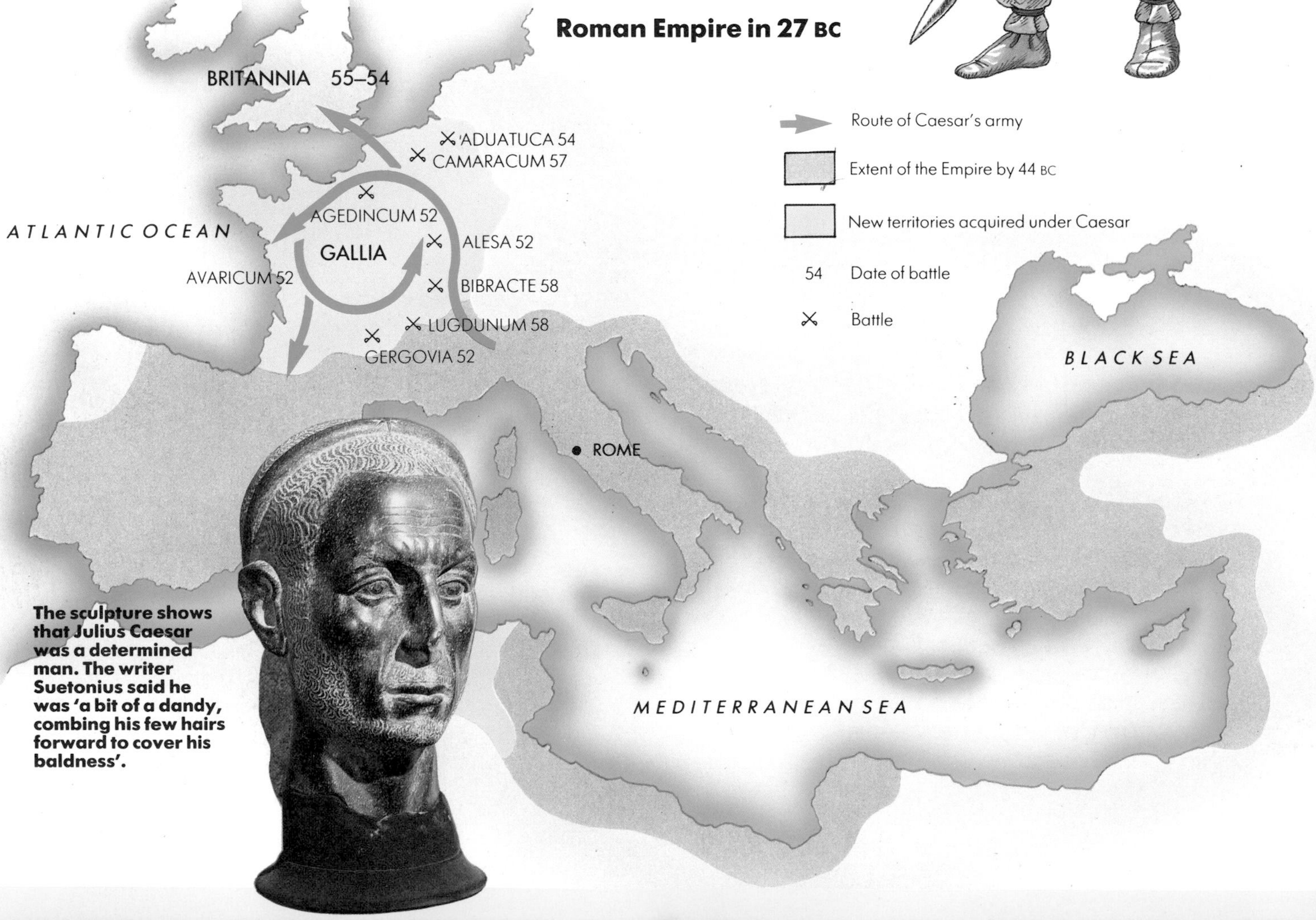

Roman Empire in 27 BC

BRITANNIA 55–54

×'ADUATUCA 54
× CAMARACUM 57

× AGEDINCUM 52

ATLANTIC OCEAN

GALLIA

× ALESA 52

AVARICUM 52

× BIBRACTE 58

× LUGDUNUM 58

GERGOVIA 52

BLACK SEA

Route of Caesar's army

Extent of the Empire by 44 BC

New territories acquired under Caesar

54   Date of battle

×   Battle

• ROME

The sculpture shows that Julius Caesar was a determined man. The writer Suetonius said he was 'a bit of a dandy, combing his few hairs forward to cover his baldness'.

MEDITERRANEAN SEA

This marble statue of the Emperor Augustus shows him at the age of 45 in the full uniform of a Roman general. On his breast plate is pictured the sun god Apollo whom Augustus regarded as his special protector.

other territories were occupied by peoples who were hostile to us or could not be trusted. Caesar has fought very successfully against the fiercest of peoples in great battles and made them part of the Roman state.

INVADING BRITAIN During his campaigns, Caesar invaded the island of Britain twice, in 55 and 54 BC. He felt that the tribes there were helping the people in northern Gaul, allowing safe refuge for campaigns across the Channel. In his first invasion in 55 BC he landed somewhere near Deal in Kent with about 12,000 troops and forced the chieftains there to accept the authority of Rome and promise not to give help to his enemies in Gaul.

This silver coin shows Julius Caesar in 44 BC.

The next year he invaded again with about 37,000 men and got as far as Hertfordshire, 40 miles from London, defeating a powerful tribe there. He did not leave any troops in Britain but he had made the new province of northern Gaul a safer part of the Roman state.

The information Caesar collected was useful to the Emperor Claudius when he decided to invade and conquer Britain in AD 43.

AFTER JULIUS CAESAR After the murder of Julius Caesar, his adopted son, Octavian, eventually vanquished all his enemies and became the most powerful man in Rome. In 27 BC he was given the special title of Augustus by the Roman senate. He governed on his own as emperor and his new name, Augustus, became the official name for emperor after that.

GOVERNING THE PROVINCES Augustus was careful to choose people he could trust to govern the provinces and be in command of the armies there. He allowed the senate to choose the governors of a few provinces, but all the rest had his own friends as governors. One very rich country, Egypt, he kept just for himself.

By Augustus' death in AD 14 the Roman state, or Empire as it can now be called, included all the lands and seas from Spain to Syria, from the Rivers Rhine and Danube to the Sahara Desert.

TRADE IN THE ROMAN EMPIRE

Small ferry boats like this unloaded cargo from ships moored in the harbor. This boat, called the Isis Giminiana, is being loaded with grain under the watchful eye of the 'magister' (the captain) named Farnaces.

The map on this page shows how vast the Roman Empire had become by the second century AD. Somewhere between 50 and 60 million people lived inside Rome's frontiers. People needed to travel within the Empire for different reasons – legions to guard the frontiers and keep down revolts, governors and their staff to administer the provinces and traders to sell their goods. The people and goods moving from place to place needed good roads and routes of communication. The Romans created both.

ROADS AND COURIERS The first roads in a new province were constructed by the army. The routes were direct and the roads as straight as possible, at least in stretches. The Emperor Augustus established an official courier service, called the *cursus publicus*, to carry official documents. There were also official 'hotels' for travellers on public business on all major routes throughout the Empire.

TRAVELING BY SHIP Although a great deal of produce was carried on land by carts and camels, much heavier loads could more easily be transported by ship. The trade in corn for bread was probably the most important of all. Vast quantities of corn were shipped from Egypt and North Africa. Huge amounts were needed to keep the poor in the city of Rome from rioting – there were 200,000 poor people registered for free food handouts by 2 BC.

Large merchant ships traded all over the Mediterranean Sea. Heavy pottery storage jars called *amphorae* were used for olive oil, wine and fish sauce. A ship might carry as many as 6000 amphorae. But it was not just food which was transported. There were materials like stone and wood for building, metal for tools, horses for the army and haulage, and wild animals for the bloody spectacles in the *amphitheater*. These, as well as luxury items such as silks, came from all over the Roman Empire and beyond – from as far away as India and China.

One interesting cargo was discovered by archaeologists working at Kenchreae near Corinth in the Roman province of Greece. They found wooden crates containing a special type of marble flooring, called *opus sectile*, inside. It was in sections, laid on a backing of plaster, resin and pieces of broken amphorae – ready made to lay down. Because of an earthquake recorded at Kenchreae in AD 375 we know when the work was supposed to have been carried out.

SAFE HARBORS AND PORTS Throughout the Roman world engineers and builders constructed harbors for all this trade. The most important was at Ostia about 15 miles from Rome. It was here that Rome's River Tiber flowed out to sea. It had been a base for the Roman navy until the reign of the Emperor Augustus.

The Emperor Claudius began the work to create a new harbor near the little port of Ostia. He even established a detachment of firemen to protect the port. This *corpus vigilum* was part of the military organization of the Roman state, and as well as fighting fires it provided police protection at night.

In AD 103 Emperor Trajan made Claudius' harbor even bigger and connected it to Ostia by a deep channel.

By the second century AD, about 50,000 people lived in Ostia. Shipping firms established themselves there and built great warehouses for the goods which passed through the port.

Sixty-one of the wealthy shipping merchants and other trades connected with shipping built a chamber of commerce for themselves.

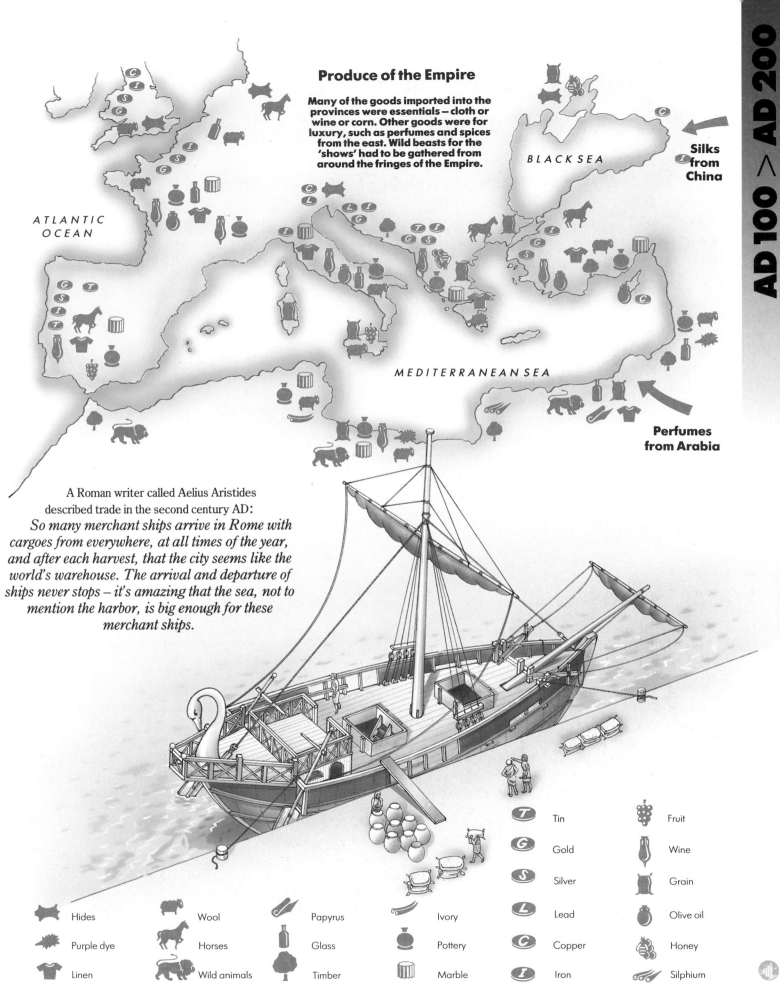

Produce of the Empire

Many of the goods imported into the provinces were essentials — cloth or wine or corn. Other goods were for luxury, such as perfumes and spices from the east. Wild beasts for the 'shows' had to be gathered from around the fringes of the Empire.

BLACK SEA

Silks from China

ATLANTIC OCEAN

MEDITERRANEAN SEA

Perfumes from Arabia

A Roman writer called Aelius Aristides described trade in the second century AD:

So many merchant ships arrive in Rome with cargoes from everywhere, at all times of the year, and after each harvest, that the city seems like the world's warehouse. The arrival and departure of ships never stops — it's amazing that the sea, not to mention the harbor, is big enough for these merchant ships.

Hides	Wool	Papyrus	Ivory
Purple dye	Horses	Glass	Pottery
Linen	Wild animals	Timber	Marble

T	Tin		Fruit
G	Gold		Wine
S	Silver		Grain
L	Lead		Olive oil
C	Copper		Honey
I	Iron		Silphium

25

PEOPLE OF THE ROMAN WORLD

Longinus's tombstone is typical of those made for cavalry officers in the Roman Empire. The top of the stone shows a sphinx – a mythical creature part winged lion, part woman. On each side is a lion entwined with a snake.

Reading the Inscriptions

Here are some examples of Latin abbreviations to help you with the tombstones on these pages:
D M – short for DIS MANIBUS means 'To the Gods of the Dead.'
H S E – short for HIC SITUS EST means

'He lies buried here.'
FECIT – means 'made,' that is put up the tombstone.
VIX – short for VIXIT means 'lived.'

1 Julia Velva from Rome buried in York

2 Longinus from Bulgaria buried in Colchester
3 Titus from Hungary buried in Rome
4 Regina from Hertfordshire buried at South Shields.
5 Husband Barathes from Palmyra buried at South Shields.
6 Vergilius from Rome buried in Rome.

A passer-by in one of the graveyards in Rome might have noticed these words on a tombstone:

Stranger, my message is short. Stand here and read it. Here is the unlovely tomb of a lovely woman. Her parents gave her the name of Claudia. She loved her husband with all her heart. She bore two sons, one of whom she leaves on earth, the other she has placed under the earth. She was charming to talk to and gentle to be with. She looked after the house and spun wool. That's my last word. Go on your way.

As we do today, the Romans often put information about the dead person on their tombstone. This one does not say how old Claudia was when she died, but others can tell us a lot about Roman people – if you can understand the code behind the words and the sculpture. Look at the pictures of tombstones on the right and read on.

JULIA VELVA The scene shown on this tombstone found in York in northern Britain is quite common. It pictures

the ceremonial feast at the burial of the dead woman who is reclining on a couch holding a glass. Food for this feast is laid out on the three-legged table in front of her. Above the scene are two pine cones which were usually burnt at funerals to give off a rich sweet-smelling odor.

The inscription under the sculpture tells us more. We see her name is Julia Velva and that she 'lived most dutifully for 50 years.' The person who inherited her property is called Aurelius Mercurialis, perhaps her son-in-law. He is standing on the right. His wife is seated on the left and the little boy is probably Julia's grandson.

LONGINUS Also buried in Britain is this junior officer (DVPLICARIUS on the tombstone) from a cavalry regiment, who died in the town of Colchester. He belonged to a squadron from the district of Sardica which is now in Bulgaria. He was the son of Sdapezematygus and died at the age of 40 after serving 15 years in the army.

Right. Julia Velva's tombstone shows a typical scene: the funeral feast. Even today many peoples have the same tradition after the burial. Scenes like this provide lots of evidence about the Romans. Look at the details of clothes, hairstyles and furniture.

Above. The inscription on the tombstone of Titus tells us that two friends, who were his heirs, put up the stone for him. They were Titus Flavius Marcellinus, a standard bearer, and Titus Aurelius Secundinus.

Right. On the far left of Vergilius' tomb you can see the bread being baked in an oven. Originally on this monument, but not shown here, were relief sculptures of Vergilius and his wife.

Above. The tombstone of Regina is unusual because it was carved in the style of her husband's place of origin – Palmyra in Syria. It is possible that it was carved by a stonemason who came from Palmyra. From the carving on the tombstone we can also see that Regina wove cloth. The inscription about her is carved in Latin but the last line is Palmyrene script.

The carving is interesting for two reasons. It was very common for a cavalry officer to have this picture showing him riding over the cowering body of a naked Celtic warrior. The other interesting thing is that the tombstone has been damaged – in Roman times. Longinus has had his face broken off. We know that this happened during the revolt of Queen Boudica against Roman rule in AD 60.

TITUS The dead person shown on this tombstone is reclining on a couch while a man leads his horse away below. His full name was Titus Aurelius Saturninus. He is an EQ SING – an *eques singularis*, a member of the mounted bodyguard for the emperor. He was born in the province of Pannonia (now Hungary) and had died at the age of 30 in Rome after serving 11 years in the army.

REGINA Regina died at the age of 30 (AN XXX) at the Roman town of Corstopitum, now Corbridge, just south of Hadrian's Wall in northern Britain. She had been bought as a slave and came from the southern tribe of the Catuvellauni whose chief town was Verulamium, now St Albans in Hertfordshire.

Her husband, who freed his wife, had this tombstone carved for her. His name was Barathes and he came from Palmyra, a very wealthy city in the Syrian desert. Barathes was also buried in Corstopitum.

VERGILIUS EURYACES Standing now just outside one of the gates of Rome put up by the Emperor Claudius is this impressive monument. It is the tomb of Vergilius Euryaces, a wealthy baker who died in 30 BC. He also provided supplies for the state, including bread for the poor of Rome.

The large holes you can see represent the standard-size containers which bakers used for measuring out flour. The frieze along the top shows Vergilius overseeing the workers in his factory making dough out of flour.

LIVING IN A ROMAN TOWN

Above top. A Roman housewife is ordering meat at the butcher's using the shopping list on her wax tablet. Notice the scales to weigh the meat.

Above. Two trades are pictured here. On the left is a ropemaker. On the right a shoemaker works in front of his cupboard with a range of shoes and sandals on top.

Roman towns were busy, noisy, bustling places. One Roman writer, Juvenal, said the streets were, *jammed with carts, crowded with people pushing and shoving, pavements and roads filthy to walk on.*

HOUSES AND FLATS Most people lived in small apartments in blocks of flats or above their shops or workshops. In Rome these blocks might be six stories high. In other places the buildings were only two stories high. Apartment blocks were usually built of wood, at least above the ground floor, and there were often serious fires in towns. Some towns had their own fire service, complete with fire crews and pumps.

Those in towns who could afford it lived in houses. They were kept private from the noisy streets by few windows and inner courtyards to keep the rooms cool and airy during the summer. Unlike the cramped flats, these houses gave the families and their slaves who lived in them complete privacy.

IN THE STREET Where it was possible, streets in Roman towns had stone or gravel surfaces and had pavements. Although there were no supermarkets, shopping was easy because you went to a particular district or street to buy goods. The leather workers, for example, would be all in one street, shops selling jugs and plates in another.

Of course there were no large panes of glass for shop windows then, so Roman shops opened on to the street. A shopkeeper might advertise with a shop sign or a notice painted on the outside wall. All towns had restaurants and take-out food bars. The most common was called a *popina*.

Some goods, such as wine in its great storage jars called *amphorae* were brought into towns from outside. Most things were made on the premises. At the baker's you could watch the flour being ground, made into dough and baked in the ovens. A blacksmith would make you a kitchen knife, or repair one on the spot.

GOING TO SCHOOL If you were up and about at dawn you would see boys and girls going off to school. There were usually more boys than girls because some parents did not believe that it was important to educate their daughters. A teacher, called a *magister ludi*, set up a school in a room somewhere, perhaps near a public square. Children from the age of seven attended schools

'How can anyone sleep in lodgings here? It's only the rich who get any sleep. The noise of the carts thundering along the narrow streets and the language of the drivers when they get stuck in a traffic jam would wake even the heaviest sleeper.' The writer Juvenal expresses the thoughts of many people who had to live in the middle of town.

like this and there was strict discipline, with a beating if they did not pay enough attention.

After five years children went on to a secondary school run by a teacher called a *grammaticus*. Here the children learned about the literature of the Romans and the Greeks, history, arithmetic, geometry and astronomy.

A few pupils, usually boys, went on to complete their education with professors who offered lessons and discussions. The boy's family could choose from several towns to send their son to receive this higher education. One of the favorite places was Athens, Greece. The Greeks already had a number of centers of education long before the Roman period and the Romans admired Greek literature and art. The Roman lawyer and politician Cicero spent two years at various 'universities.'

Roman Writing

Fragments of Roman writing can be seen in many museums today. But these are usually in the form of inscriptions carved on stone. Handwriting is less common because it is harder to preserve. You can sometimes find names, words or phrases scratched on to roof tiles, and graffiti on walls. For example, a worker in a tile factory in Roman London wrote this about his workmate, 'Austalis has been skiving off by himself every day for the last thirteen days!'

In a Roman school

Writing instruments and 'paper' in the form of a wax tablet and rolls of papyrus. The inkwell can be hung up to be used more easily.

or office you would find writing on three types of material. Papyrus was made into scrolls from the leaves of a plant that grows near rivers, especially in Egypt. Pens and ink were used on papyrus. Wax tablets were shallow wooden boxes filled with wax. Romans used a sharp metal point called a stylus to scratch out their words.

Little 'notebooks' were made from very thin pieces of wood, joined together with leather thongs, which were written on with pens and ink.

ROME: CAPITAL OF THE EMPIRE

Part of the main forum in Rome, called the Forum Romanum. On the left are the remaining columns of the Temple of the god Saturn.

Anyone living inside the Roman Empire would expect to see towns in all the provinces with much the same facilities. It was all part of being *civilized*. When new towns were built in the provinces, the townspeople would want the sorts of buildings and amenities they had seen, or heard about, in the capital of the Empire – Rome.

THE BEGINNINGS OF A CITY It was under the Etruscan kings that the various villages became the single town of Rome on the west bank of the River Tiber. By the time of Julius Caesar there were nearly one million people living on the seven hills of Rome and in the valleys leading down to the river.

In the city center there were buildings for government, religion, trade and entertainment.

PUBLIC SERVICES The Romans were good at

engineering and from the earliest periods laid out good routes of communication. Major roads led out from the city center to other parts of Italy. A good water supply was essential, especially for such a huge population. Great stone *aqueducts* carried water in channels over arches across the city. The first aqueduct was built by the politician Appius Claudius in 312 BC and named after him, the *Aqua Appia*. Each town needed an official, called a *curator aquarum*, to look after the water supply.

Water was brought to public fountains and tanks alongside main streets to supply people and industries. It was also needed in huge quantities for the public baths. Each town had at least one major bath where large numbers of people could enjoy the various forms of bathing – hot, steamy rooms, cold pools and saunas, as well as exercise halls.

THE FORUM At the center of the town was the *forum*.

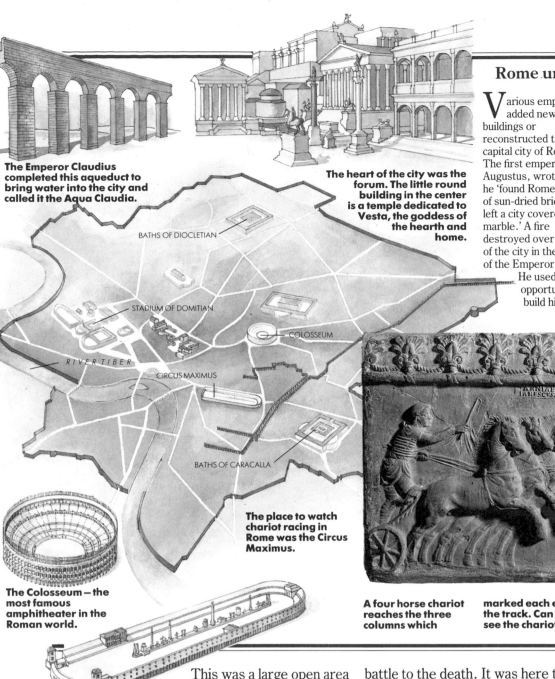

The Emperor Claudius completed this aqueduct to bring water into the city and called it the Aqua Claudia.

The heart of the city was the forum. The little round building in the center is a temple dedicated to Vesta, the goddess of the hearth and home.

BATHS OF DIOCLETIAN

STADIUM OF DOMITIAN

COLOSSEUM

RIVER TIBER

CIRCUS MAXIMUS

BATHS OF CARACALLA

The place to watch chariot racing in Rome was the Circus Maximus.

The Colosseum – the most famous amphitheater in the Roman world.

Rome under the Emperors

Various emperors added new buildings or reconstructed the capital city of Rome. The first emperor, Augustus, wrote that he 'found Rome built of sun-dried bricks but left a city covered in marble.' A fire destroyed over a third of the city in the reign of the Emperor Nero. He used the opportunity to build himself a splendid palace in a huge park. New areas were needed for political gatherings, religious ceremonies and markets. There were six major public baths in the city center. By the third century AD the city had expanded into its seven surrounding hills and a wall was built to encircle it and the camp of the city's guards.

A four horse chariot reaches the three columns which marked each end of the track. Can you see the charioteer ahead just turning the corner?

This was a large open area where markets could take place and the people could carry on the business of the town. Around the forum were the buildings for the government of the town, and in Rome itself, for the government of the state. Public halls, called *basilicas*, with aisles on each side of the long building, were used for law courts and public meetings. The forum was also the place where you would find temples to the gods of the city and the most important of the Roman gods and goddesses.

PLACES FOR ENTERTAINMENT A Roman might tell you that any decent town would be able to provide the people who lived there some public entertainment. There were three very popular forms of entertainment in the Roman world. The most popular took place in the *amphitheater*. In these huge oval-shaped stadiums as many as 50,000 spectators watched trained fighters called *gladiators*

battle to the death. It was here too that gladiators would hunt and hope to kill wild beasts, such as lions, bears, deer, elephants and snakes.

The bloodthirsty spectators also enjoyed watching convicted criminals fight to the death or be torn apart by wild animals. Sometimes amphitheatres were flooded to recreate sea battles.

Theaters were for smaller audiences. As many as 5,000 people might watch a series of Greek or Roman plays lasting all day. There were other types of performances though, including the *mimus* which was a short sketch, and the *pantomimus* which was a sort of ballet with music.

Finally there was the thrill of watching chariot racing in the *circus*. The biggest of all was the Circus Maximus in Rome. In the first century BC it could hold 100,000 people, but by the fourth century AD it had been enlarged to a capacity of 350,000!

LIVING ON A
COUNTRY ESTATE

You may have come across the Latin word *villa* before. Today it is often used to mean a countryside or seaside house where you spend your vacations. The Romans used the word villa for the same thing, but it also meant a farm.

RICH LANDOWNERS If you were wealthy enough to afford more than one house, you would be able to choose which of your houses to spend your time in. You might say, like the Roman poet Martial, 'Whenever I'm worn out with worry and want to get some rest, I go to my villa.' Country houses with farming land brought in a great deal of wealth for some people. The houses the wealthy built for themselves on their farming estates were often grand and certainly had the facilities required

for gracious living – courtyards with covered walks, formal gardens, bath houses and several dining rooms. The Romans had a special name for the owner's house on a farming estate – the *villa urbana*.

THE WORKING FARM BUILDINGS Many people who owned large farms chose not to live on them all through the year. When this happened they employed a farm manager, called a *vilicus*, to look after the work. The house of the farm manager was called a *villa rustica*. If the farm manager was married, his wife was probably also employed on the farm as the *vilica* – that is the manager, or housekeeper in charge of the household slaves. The vilicus and the vilica would probably be slaves, too.

Gaius Plinius to his dear friend Gallus: *Greetings! You are amazed that I am so fond of my Villa at Laurentum. You won't be when you see how charming it is – on a fine stretch of seashore and only seventeen miles from Rome. I can spend the night here after a full day's work in the city.*

LETTER OF PLINY

Villas often grew a variety of produce as well as breeding animals. On the right oxen are pulling a cart full of baskets of fruit. On the left is an area in the farmyard set aside for large storage jars. These jars, called amphorae, stored the harvest of wine or olive oil. Later the produce or animals were taken to local markets or shipped direct to Rome itself.

All the other farm buildings were given the name *villa fructuaria*, which literally means the places where produce was kept.

One Roman writer, Columella, tells us that there should be *'rooms for oil, for the oil presses, for wine, for hay-lofts, granaries and storage places for wine and oil ready to go to the market.'* In some parts of the Empire the farming estates produced one main crop, such as wheat.

FARM WORKERS Those who worked on large farms were usually slaves. The work was very hard and the hours long. The farm manager had to be tough to control a workforce like this.

Besides the work needed to plant and harvest the produce on the farm or look after the animals, a villa needed to be as self-sufficient as possible. They obviously tried to grow all the food they needed for the workforce but other jobs, such as maintaining buildings and machinery, were also carried out by the slaves. Often travelling craftspeople would come to the farm to offer special skills such as pottery, tile making or ironworking.

This mosaic from Tunisia in north Africa shows the house of the owner – the villa urbana – with its towers and colonnades. In the foreground are ducks on the edge of a pond, geese and pheasants. Surrounding the villa are fruit trees, bushes and roses.

The house of the villa owner – the *villa urbana* – often contained parts which were similar to town houses, like this one from Pompeii. This is the garden of the House of the Vetii brothers which had all the latest styles of decoration. In a typical *villa urbana* the garden would have been in front of the house.

RELIGION AND THE GODS OF THE ROMAN WORLD

Religion was a very important part of people's lives in Roman times. They believed that their gods and goddesses and spirits surrounded them and controlled everything they did. They even treated the emperors as gods. People believed that they had to make sacrifices and offerings to keep the gods and spirits friendly. There were altars and statues everywhere – not only inside temples but in the streets and in houses too.

This list of sacrifices from a document found at Dura-Europus in the Roman province of Syria shows how important sacrifices and ceremonies were to the military garrison stationed there in AD 224:

January 3. Our vows fulfilled and offered for the preservation of our lord Emperor Marcus Aurelius Severus Alexander Augustus and for the eternity of the Empire of the Roman people. Sacrificed to Jupiter Best and Greatest, an ox; to Juno, a cow; to Minerva, a cow; to Jupiter Victor, an ox; to Father Mars, a bull; to Victory, a cow . . .

January 24. Birthday of the deified Emperor Hadrian. Sacrificed to the deified Hadrian, an ox.

TEMPLES AND PROCESSIONS The Romans believed

Above. Sculpture found on Hadrian's Wall showing the birth of the god Mithras from an egg. Around him are the signs of the zodiac.
Right. The Roman town of Sufetula (now Sbeitla) in Tunisia. Through the arch you can see the impressive front of the Temple of Jupiter.
Below right. Statue of Diana, the woodland goddess of hunting, now in Istanbul (Constantinople).

that their gods and goddesses took human forms and had special responsibilities. For example, Juno was the patron goddess of women. They built temples for their gods and a priest, called a *pontifex*, carried out ceremonies and sacrifices on behalf of the worshippers. The ceremony might involve a procession through the town ending in the sacrifice of animals at the altar of the temple.

LIFE AFTER DEATH The Romans believed in a life after death. The dead went to the underworld to live with the *manes*, the gods of the dead.

Offerings were made to the gods by pouring out wine or leaving food such as honey cakes at the grave side. These ceremonies were held nine days after burial and then at special times throughout the year.

GODS FROM OTHER COUNTRIES As the Romans conquered more and more territories they came into contact with other gods and goddesses. Most of these new figures they adopted into their own 'family' of gods. Some of them became very important gods to the Romans. For example, the Egyptian goddess Isis and the god Serapis were both worshipped all over the Empire. The Persian god Mithras had temples built for him by soldiers and merchants in most provinces.

CHRISTIANITY Not all foreign religions were liked or accepted by the Romans. They outlawed the worship of the Druids, which took place in Britain and in Gaul and involved human sacrifice. There were several wars with the Jews. Christianity was practiced secretly in many parts of the Empire. Christians were persecuted and often massacred in amphitheaters.

In the end, Christianity survived and was made the official religion of Rome by the Emperor Constantine I in AD 312. However many Romans still went on worshipping the other gods.

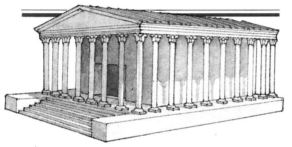

Temples of the Romans

Various types of temples were built by the Romans. The first (top) was designed like Greek temples. Built on a platform it had an imposing front entrance. Columns lined the front and sides of the building inside, called the *cella*. Sometimes temples were enclosed in a sacred courtyard area (middle) called a *temenos*. Statues and altars would be put up here and ceremonies and processions held inside its walls.

In Gaul and in Britain a different type of temple (bottom) was often built. This is known as a Romano-Celtic

temple because it was built for the Celtic gods and goddesses adopted by the Romans. The *cella* of this type of temple is surrounded by a colonnaded terrace. They were sometimes built inside a *temenos*.

Roman Gods and Goddesses

Venus was the goddess of beauty and love. Julius Caesar built her a temple in Rome because he claimed to be a descendant of the hero Aeneas, who was the son of the divine Mars (god of war) and Venus.

Bacchus (also called **Dionysus**) was a god who was worshipped by the Greeks. He was a god of fertility, especially of the fruit of trees. This included grapes which made wine. He is often shown drinking, as here.

Diana, the goddess of hunting, is usually pictured hunting with bow and arrows. She was worshipped as a goddess of fertility in wooded places. She was also one of the goddesses associated with women.

Juno was the most important goddess of women and the wife of Jupiter. In early Roman times she was only associated with childbirth. Later she became one of the main goddesses of the Roman state.

Mercury was the Roman god of traders and merchants. His Greek counterpart is the god Hermes. Hermes was the messenger god and, like Mercury, is usually shown with a winged helmet and sandals.

Jupiter, the king of all the gods, is shown here on his throne with his emblem — the eagle. The eagle was adopted by the Roman state as their symbol of power. Zeus is his Greek counterpart.

GUARDING THE FRONTIERS
OF THE EMPIRE

You have read how the Romans needed a large army to conquer their Empire. It was just as important to have a large force to control it and keep their enemies outside its limits. In the second century AD, when there were between 50 and 60 million people living in the Roman Empire, there were only about 450,000 soldiers in the army.

FRONTIERS OF THE EMPIRE About 28,000 of these soldiers were on patrol in the province of Africa which supplied Rome with an enormous amount of grain. Here, as in other provinces, there was a network of good roads and strong permanent forts. The Roman emperors tried to establish frontiers wherever they could. In the deserts of Arabia and Syria, the Emperor Trajan built a large number of roads and forts to form the easternmost boundary of the Empire.

In the north there was a need for more permanent frontiers to keep out the *barbarians*, as uncivilized neighbors were called. A permanent barrier, called the *limes*, of a bank, a ditch, and a wooden fence with watch towers and forts, was constructed between the River Rhine and the Danube. On the northern edge of Roman territory in Britain, the Emperor Hadrian had a stone wall constructed – known now as Hadrian's Wall.

Roman soldiers had more to do than just fight the enemy. A legionary soldier would often find himself on regular patrol but would also have to guard important

This fine stretch of Hadrian's Wall shows one of the guard posts built at every mile. Gates allowed civilians and soldiers to pass through this frontier line.

places such as quarries and mines or act as customs officer at frontier crossing points. There were other jobs too as these records from a legion posted to Egypt in about AD 80 show:

Titus Flavius Valens . . . assigned to papyrus manufacture January 15, returned. Assigned to coin mint January 17, returned. Assigned to the granary at Mercurium . . .

THE PERMANENT FORT The size of a fort depended on the size of the army unit based there. Some forts were enormous and could house an entire legion of about 6,000 men. As you would expect, the forts were laid out in a very regular way with streets between buildings to give easy and quick access to the surrounding ramparts and walls. Strongly built and defended gateways and guard towers were placed on the walls. The barrack buildings were long and put together in groups. In the center was the headquarters building for the commander-in-chief and his officers. It was here that the administration of the unit was carried out, and here the pay and the standards of the unit were kept safely.

Other buildings inside the fort would include granaries and storehouses, cookhouses and lavatories, workshops and a hospital and sometimes the commander's own house. Outside there might be a bath house for the troops.

Beyond the walls of the permanent forts a civilian settlement usually grew up. The Romans called this the *canabae*. Roman soldiers were not allowed to marry and have families while on active duty, although many did. Shops and other services for soldiers, such as taverns, were a regular feature of canabae.

DOCUMENTS AND LETTERS Out of the pay a soldier received from the army he had to pay for his food and clothes. We know that army units had to keep a careful account of supplies sent in to the fort. Two records recently discovered at the fort of Vindolanda on Hadrian's Wall give a list of items delivered: *barley, Celtic beer, wine, fish-sauce, pork-fat, spices, salt, young pig, ham, wheat, venison, roe-deer . . .*

Perhaps even more interesting was this letter which has partly survived on the wooden backing of a wax tablet, also from Vindolanda:

I have sent you . . . pairs of woollen socks, two pairs of sandals and two pairs of underpants . . .

Each fort was laid out so that the soldiers could reach any section quickly. The best troops were next to the main gate so that they could charge out against the enemy.

The headquarters building of the fort.

Forts and Soldiers

The soldier on the left is a legionary soldier. He is carrying a javelin and a short stabbing sword. He is well protected by his armor. His helmet has cheek pieces and a neck guard. His body armor is made of plates of metal hinged together to allow him to move easily. His groin is protected by an apron of metal discs riveted on to leather straps. His shield is wooden with a layer of linen or leather on the outside and a bronze or iron center boss.

On a march in hostile territory the army would build a camp each night. It was the same layout

Above. Barracks for the soldiers were built in pairs opening out onto a corridor. Each barrack had 11 rooms – one for the centurion and 10 for the 80 men under his command.

as the drawing of the permanent one above. The Roman writer Josephus said, 'The inside is measured out

and streets laid down . . . It seems like a town suddenly sprung up.'

In the late first century AD there were legions guarding the north west frontier on the rivers Rhine and Danube. The other legions which made up the entire Roman army were placed in trouble spots mainly in the eastern Mediterranean, each legion had its own number and name – taken from the place where it was raised, or named after an emperor or a victory, for example LEGIO I ITALICA or LEGIO II AUGUSTA or VI VICTRIX.

THE EMPIRE COMES TO AN END

The Roman World in the Fourth and Fifth Centuries AD

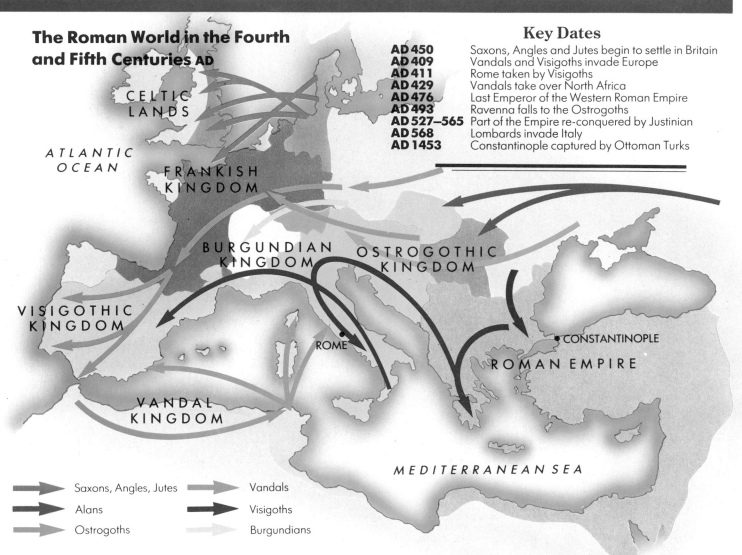

Key (map legend):
- Saxons, Angles, Jutes
- Alans
- Ostrogoths
- Vandals
- Visigoths
- Burgundians

The Roman Empire grew gradually from a town in central Italy to a world power. It was difficult to control such a huge area and even more difficult to keep out those many enemies who were waiting beyond the boundaries. Even so, the Empire maintained control for several centuries.

COASTAL ATTACKS During the third century AD there were attacks along the coasts of Britain and Gaul. A series of new forts had to be built and a strong naval force patrolled the coastline.

THE EMPIRE REORGANIZED In AD 284 the Emperor Diocletian made an important change to the way his Empire was ruled. He divided the huge Roman territory in two. He ruled the eastern part from the city of Nicomedia in Bithynia, while his friend, Maximian, ruled the western part from Rome. To help govern the Empire, Diocletian established twelve districts called *dioceses*. Each district had a governor called a *vicarius*. At the same time the army was enlarged but divided into two new groups. From now on there were permanent troops stationed on the frontiers and small mobile units which could be moved to trouble spots very quickly.

RETURN TO ONE EMPEROR The Roman Empire returned to the rule of one emperor in AD 324 when Emperor Constantine finally defeated his enemies. However he moved his capital to Constantinople (now Istanbul in Turkey) in AD 330. Constantinople was later to become Byzantium.

Below. Coin of the Emperor Diocletian who reigned from AD 284–305. He had previously been the commander of the imperial guard. He abdicated in AD 305 and retired to his fortified palace at Salona (now Split) in Yugoslavia.

Left. Most Roman traditions continued in the Eastern Empire. This is part of a fine floor mosaic laid in the imperial palace at Constantinople during the reign of Justinian. It shows two gladiators fighting wild animals in an amphitheater. Below. The head from a colossal statue of the Emperor Constantine I, called 'The Great', who reigned from AD 306–337. The statue was carved in about AD 315 in Rome.

Emperors of the Later Roman Empire

West

287–305	Maximian Augustus
293–306	Constantius I
306–307	Severus
306–337	Constantine I

East

284–305	Diocletian Augustus
293–305	Galerius
305–311	Galerius Augustus
305–313	Maximinus Augustus
308–324	Licinius
324–327	Constantine I, sole ruler of whole Empire

Above. Coin showing the Emperor Justinian who reigned from AD 527–565. The coin celebrates the victory of his general, Belisarius, over the Vandals in AD 535.

A RE-DIVIDED EMPIRE After the Emperor Theodosius in AD 395, the Empire was once again divided into two with capitals at Constantinople and Rome. The Western Empire suffered most at the hands of its enemies. Waves of barbarian tribes began to swarm over Europe, causing disruption and destruction. By the mid-fifth century the Saxons, Jutes and Angles from Belgium, Holland, Germany and southern Scandinavia had settled in eastern Britain. From the north and east, enemies such as the Visigoths and Huns began to occupy large areas of the Roman Empire. For example, the Visigoth chief Alaric took Rome itself in AD 411. The last Emperor in the west, Romulus Augustulus, only reigned from AD 475 to 476. In this year Odovacar led German armies into Italy and declared himself king.

THE EASTERN EMPIRE The rulers in Constantinople were not as hard pressed by enemies beyond their borders. In fact the Emperor Justinian in AD 527 began to re-conquer some of the old Roman Empire which had been lost to the barbarians. Justinian's armies re-occupied parts of Africa, Spain and Italy.

After Justinian's death the attacks began again and the Lombards invaded Italy in AD 568. In the late seventh century the Muslims took over Africa and then Spain. The Eastern Roman Empire, which was also known as the Byzantine Empire, continued to be ruled by emperors until AD 1453. This was the year the capital of the Eastern Empire, Constantinople, was captured by the Ottoman Turks. This signalled the fall of one of the greatest empires ever seen.

The Roman World
TIME CHART

	THE CITY OF ROME	THE ROMAN DOMAIN
BC		
752	Legendary foundation of Rome	
509	Etruscan kings thrown out Roman Republic established	
390	Gauls beseige Rome	
343>290		Wars with the Samnites
280>275		Greeks invade Italy
264>261		First war with Carthage
237>202		Second war with Carthage
149>146		Third war with Carthage
146		Carthage destroyed
133>122	Land reforms of Tiberius and Gaius Gracchus	
83>82		Civil war
49>45		Civil war
44	Julius Caesar 'Dictator for Life.' Murdered same year.	
31>29		Civil war
27	Augustus begins reign as Emperor. The Empire.	
AD		
14	Augustus dies	
43		Emperor Claudius invades Britain
80		Vesuvius erupts. Pompeii and Herculaneum destroyed.
79	Colosseum opens	
114	Emperor Trajan builds his column in Rome	
122		Hadrian's Wall begun
212		All men in provinces made citizens of Rome
284	Empire divided into two. Ruled from two capitals.	
312	Christianity made official religion of Rome	
330		Emperor Constantine moves capital of Empire to Constantinople
402		Western capital moved to Ravenna
410	Rome sacked by Visigoths	
455	Rome attacked by Vandals	
476	Last Emperor in Rome thrown out by German armies	
540	Eastern Empire forces recapture Italy	
1453		Turks capture Constantinople. Fall of the Holy Roman Empire.

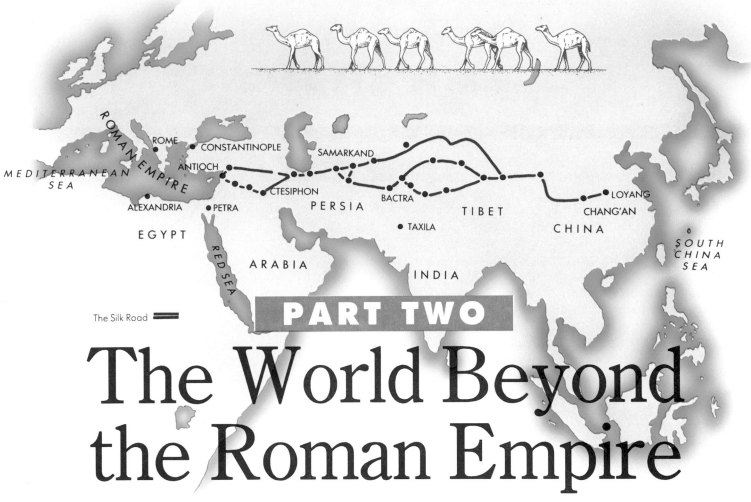

The Silk Road ▬

PART TWO

The World Beyond the Roman Empire

N ow we are going to look at the world beyond the boundaries of the Roman Empire. All the civilizations you will read about in this section have some connection with Rome – usually through trade, but sometimes because they were conquered by the Romans.

Just before he died in AD 14, the Roman Emperor Augustus deposited in the state archives a manuscript called *Res Gestae Divi Augusti*, 'The Achievements of the Divine Augustus.' In it he says:

Royal embassies from India, never seen before by any Roman general, were often sent to me.

But India was not the furthest place with which Rome was connected. Exotic goods came from as far away as China.

THE SILK ROAD The map shows the way the Far East was connected with Europe over a route known as the Silk Road. The term is odd because it was not really a road but a series of caravan routes between towns and oases. Nor did the merchants carry only silk, but a great variety of expensive goods.

Chinese silk was especially popular – if you could afford it. Fragments have been found in sixth century graves in Athens and in Iron Age burials in Germany. The Romans bought these luxury goods in large quantites. One Roman writer, called Pliny the Elder, said in the first century AD:

India, China and the Arabian states drain our Empire of a huge amount of money every year – this is what our luxuries and our women are costing us.

The trade traffic was two-way, of course. In exchange for all these luxury items from the east, the Romans must have sent gold and silver coins, fine pottery, glass vessels and precious stones.

TRAVEL OVER LAND Travel over land was dangerous and slow, at least by modern standards. Roman writers calculated that a camel train could cover about 20 miles in one day.

Very few traders covered the whole route. Most worked shorter distances passing goods on to other traders. Many places, such as Taxila (see page 60) and Petra (see page 70), became wealthy simply because of their positions as trade centers.

TRAVEL BY SEA The sea routes for trade were also extremely important. A great deal of silk came to India and from there by sea to Europe. Roman coins and objects such as pottery have been found in southern India. There was even a Roman trading station at Arikamedu on the south-eastern coast of India.

41

Life in Ancient China
THE HAN DYNASTY

The civilization of China began very early in history. By 6000 BC there were villages in China where farmers bred pigs, kept dogs and grew millet. Later soya beans and rice were introduced. We know that from 2700 BC the Chinese had discovered how to produce silk from silkworms. From about 1800 BC there were cities in China which were defended against their enemies. In these cities Chinese craftworkers were producing fine quality pottery and metal objects. After 1500 BC the Chinese had invented a system for writing.

THE EMPEROR CH'IN The Chinese cities fought each other as well as outside enemies. After centuries of civil war one man became the most powerful. He was the Emperor Ch'in Shi-huang-ti. In 221 BC he united the vast country into one Empire and gave China its name. His own family, or *dynasty*, did not rule China for very long – only 11 years – but the system of government he set up lasted until 1912.

THE GREAT WALL The Emperor Ch'in is probably best known for the massive stone wall, the Great Wall, which he built on the northern borders of China. Some of the northern states had built walls to protect themselves but Emperor Ch'in joined several together to form a unified frontier.

The Chinese Empire was divided into a number of provinces, each with its own governor and military commander.

THE HAN DYNASTY The military campaigns and costly building projects like the Great Wall made people hostile to the rule of Ch'in and a new civil war began in 210 BC. After the war a new dynasty emerged called the Han Dynasty.

The most important of China's enemies were the Xiongnu tribes to the north of the Great Wall. Under the Han Dynasty there were campaigns against these tribes. The Great Wall was extended to the northwest to protect the important trade route into central Asia. Trade with the West began at this time.

The Han Empire was also extended to the east into Korea to include those states on the edge of the South China Sea. The princes who had ruled their own small territories were gradually taken into the Empire and ruled from the capital.

CHANG'AN – CAPITAL OF CHINA The earliest surviving count of the people (called a *census*), taken in the Han Dynasty in AD 1, gives 57 million as China's population. This vast population was controlled from the capital city, which was Chang'an. The city was more like an enormous imperial court than a city. More than two-thirds of the area was taken up by royal palaces. Little now remains of the buildings of Chang'an. However, it is known that high pavilions were popular in the Han period, and a pavilion 380 feet high is said to have been built in Chang'an.

This bronze figure of a horse is typical of the fine art of the Eastern Han dynasty of the second century AD. It is only 34.5 cm high but shows the horse at a 'flying' gallop. The horse is neighing and is carefully balanced on a swallow in flight.

Han China

As early as the third century BC fortifications, mainly of earth, were built in the north to keep the 'barbarians' out of China. The Emperor Ch'in joined them together, reinforced them and made the Great Wall of China. It stretches for about 1380 miles and stands about 25 feet high with towers and defended gateways.

Key Dates

Shang Dynasty 1600–1027 BC
There were constant wars and their enemies, if captured, could be slaughtered in the royal tombs.

Zhou Dynasty 1027–771 BC
King Wu of Zhou overthrew the Shang Dynasty and established his capital at Hao-ching.

Warring States 475–221 BC
There was constant warfare in this period.

Ch'in and Western Han Dynasties 221 BC–AD 8
Emperor Ch'in united the country.

Hsin Dynasty AD 9–23
Wang Mang took control and became emperor.

Eastern Han Dynasty AD 24–220

1 The early peoples in the Andes Mountains were called Chavin and were building huge ceremonial temples from about 1200 BC. The Nazca people established themselves from about 200 BC. There is still a great mystery about the Nazca people because of the 'lines' they created. They cleared away the surface to reveal the underlying rock, making parallel lines or geometric shapes. Sometimes monkeys, birds or spiders were drawn out. Their real purpose is unknown and most can only be appreciated from the air. They may have been 'offerings' to their gods.

2 In the southwest of North America from about 1000 BC people hunted and gathered food but also practiced some small-scale farming. The climate was dry and the people are known, from what has been preserved, as the 'Basketmakers'. By AD 1 they were building very small villages with houses which had floors sunk below ground. Most of the food they ate was gathered or hunted, but some plants, like maize, were cultivated.

Map labels: CH'I, HAN-TAN, CHANG'AN, LO-YANG, YELLOW RIVER, RIVER YANGTZE, SOUTH CHINA SEA, NAN-HAI-CHUN

☐ Extent of Han Empire

☐ Kingdoms

〜 Great Wall of China

Warfare was common in ancient China. Warriors carried weapons of bronze, iron and even of bamboo. This Han helmet has been pieced together from fragments found during an excavation. It provides protection to the top of the head, and the ears.

BURIAL IN THE HAN DYNASTY

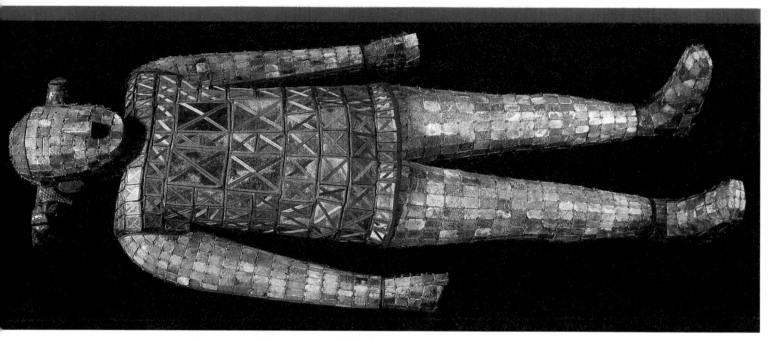

Above. The bodies of Prince Liu Sheng and his wife Tou Wan were encased in suits made from pieces of jade, which the Chinese believed prevented decay. Archaeologists found the suits collapsed but were able to reconstruct them. Right. From the first century AD pottery models of buildings were placed in tombs.

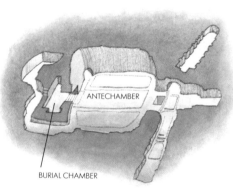

ANTECHAMBER

BURIAL CHAMBER

Left. Prince Liu Sheng and Princess Tou Wan were buried in different tombs. This is Tou Wan's tomb carved out of the solid rock. An entrance gallery on the right led to two chambers which contained beautiful objects. A main chamber led to the place of burial at the far end.

The ancient Chinese believed in a life after death. They also believed that life would be just the same after death so they took their possessions with them. In earlier dynasties the Chinese killed their servants and buried them with their dead masters and mistresses to continue to serve them in the next world. Later on, models of servants and soldiers were placed in graves.

Archaeologists have been able to discover an enormous amount about the Chinese way of life in the early periods from the burial tombs. Objects were carefully placed with the person who was buried – even food for the next world.

THE BURIAL OF THE FIRST EMPEROR Perhaps the most spectacular of the Chinese burials was that of Ch'in Shi-huang-ti. His royal tomb was discovered quite by accident in 1974 by farmers digging wells for water. At Mount Li in the Shansi province they found huge pits containing life-size models of 7000 warriors – each with a different face. They must have been modelled on the real warriors.

BURIAL IN THE HAN DYNASTY The tombs of the Han Dynasty were very elaborate. Tomb walls were often decorated with scenes of everyday life – in the kitchen, on the farm or working at industries such as salt mining.

THE PRINCE AND THE PRINCESS Two of the finest tombs ever discovered from the Han Dynasty are those of Prince Liu Sheng and his wife the Princess Tou Wan. The tombs were discovered at Mancheng which is 90 miles south-west of Beijing (Peking). Archaeologists,

The tomb of Emperor Ch'in Shi-huang-ti:
• was discovered in March 1974 at Mount Li by farmers digging a well for water
• was under a huge mound of earth 1680 yards square
• contained 7000 warriors, 3000 footsoldiers, six chariots with horses as well as bowmen, spearmen and officers
• took about 700,000 forced laborers 36 years to build.

The tombs of Liu Sheng and Tou Wan:
• were discovered in June 1968 at Mancheng when soldiers fell into a hole that led underground
• were sealed under a layer of molten iron
• contained over 2800 objects which included the burial suits. Tou Wan's suit had 2156 jade pieces sewn together with over 24 ounces of gold wire.

Part of the tomb of China's first emperor, Ch'in Shi-huang-ti showing some of the 7000 pottery models of warriors. Also buried are pottery horses and chariots.

local people and soldiers took months to clear the passageways and chambers of the two tombs. All the hard work was worth it – the tombs had lain untouched since they were built in 113 BC.

CONSTRUCTING THE TOMB Prince Liu Sheng, who was the brother of the Emperor Wu-ti, had ordered the tombs to be built before his death. They were cut into the hillside out of solid rock. Not only was there a special chamber for each of the bodies of the Prince and Princess but there were three other chambers and long entrance passageways.

There was always the danger of tomb-robbing in ancient China so the Prince had taken special precautions. On his own tomb he had the walls sealed with rocks and molten iron.

BURIED WITH THE DEAD Inside the two tombs the archaeologists found more than 2800 objects. There were jars to hold food and wine; gold and bronze vessels, weapons, lamps, incense burners and little figures of animals. One particularly interesting find was a collection of figures of acrobats, musicians and spectators.

BURIAL SUITS OF JADE The bodies of the Prince and Princess were placed in carefully made suits of jade. Jade is a very hard semi-precious stone. Each suit was made from over 2000 small tablets of jade held together with gold wire.

As the bodies inside rotted away, the suits collapsed. Archaeologists constructed dummies of the right size and reconstructed the suits around them so that we can see what they would have looked like.

ART AND CRAFTS OF THE HAN DYNASTY

Industry and trade were important in the Han Dynasty. Two of the most important industries – ironworking and salt production – were controlled by the state.

MAKING IRON The production of iron was made a state industry in 119 BC. The ancient Chinese were well ahead of the rest of the world in their knowledge of iron. Cast iron (that is poured into a mold) had been made since about 500 BC. Cast iron was not used in the western world until the Industrial Revolution in the nineteenth century.

Iron ore had to be dug from the ground, then melted at very high temperatures. The Chinese ironworkers used charcoal, and later, coal to heat the ore. We know that in the Han Dynasty there were 49 blast furnaces to produce cast iron. The furnaces were built of heat resistant bricks.

The Chinese of the Han period could make an even harder type of iron – steel. They did this by introducing carbon into the cast iron. Chinese archaeologists have excavated a number of iron furnaces and experimented on the site of one at Wenxian.

OBJECTS MADE OF IRON Iron could be used for all sorts of objects. At Wenxian the furnaces produced vast quantities of belt buckles and horse harness fittings. Weapons, tools and parts of ploughs and other objects for farming were also made of iron.

ART AND CRAFTS You have read about Han burials. The tombs contained the best evidence we have for the quality of craftwork in ancient China. Artists worked in bronze and gold with inlays of other metals and stone.

LACQUERWORK *Lacquerwork* objects have been found from before the Han period. Lacquer is a substance which comes from the tree called *Rhus verniciflua* which only grows in the Far East. A coating of lacquer will seal an object and preserve it. Lacquer also gives a brilliant shine to an object and brings out the colors. Wooden objects such as bowls, trays, boxes and even room screens were lacquered.

PICTURES FROM THE PAST Much of our detailed evidence for daily life comes from wall paintings and engravings in tombs. Favorite scenes are kitchens, with details of food preparation, and banquets. We can learn more about what the ancient Chinese ate from the detailed lists recorded in tombs and the labels put onto the food containers.

In the Han period the most common foods were: rice and flour noodles; soup with meat and vegetables; vegetables – lotus roots, soya beans, leeks, yams, bamboo shoots, radishes; fruits – melons, plums, oranges, mandarins, peaches, pears, apricots, water chestnuts; meat – horse, dog, wild boar, beef, lamb, hare, chicken and game; spices and flavorings – sugar, honey, garlic, onion, cinnamon, ginger, salt, vinegar, soya sauce; drinks – milk, beer, also drinks made from fruits like plums.

Made during the Han period, these lacquerwork boxes show obedient sons and daughters along their sides.

The Chinese had to become skilled in cavalry fighting to defeat the nomads in the north. This influenced the artists who produced heads like this one of jade, as well as decorated horse trappings.

Below. The decoration on this horse harness made of bronze is of an elk. The idea of this sort of decoration came from the nomadic tribes in the Ordos region north of the Great Wall of China.

Above. A pottery model of a ferocious-looking guard or hunting dog. You can see the strong breast strap and the eye for attaching the lead. Other animals were often subjects for these little models, which were placed in tombs. One strange creature looked like a cross between a rhinoceros and a hippopotamus.

One of the many objects found buried with the Princess Tou Wan (see page 44). This shows the head of a servant girl, made of bronze. It is part of a little statue of the girl who is holding a lamp.

Silk Weaving

Silk is a fiber which comes from the cocoon of the silkworm. The silkworm feeds on the leaves of the mulberry tree and is 'farmed.' The drawing on the right shows the silkworms feeding on leaves placed on racks.

The larvae of the silkworms grow to about 3 inches in length after five weeks of eating mulberry leaves. Then they begin to spin their cocoons. Each cocoon is made up of two continuous fiber threads, about 1000 yards in length, stuck together with a gum called seracin. To remove the silk fiber the cocoons are softened in hot water in a vat and the cocoons are unwound. They can then be twisted together ready to be woven.

The very fine silk was then woven into cloth on a loom. Garments made of silk were very fashionable and expensive in the Han period, as they are today.

LANGUAGE AND WRITING
IN ANCIENT CHINA

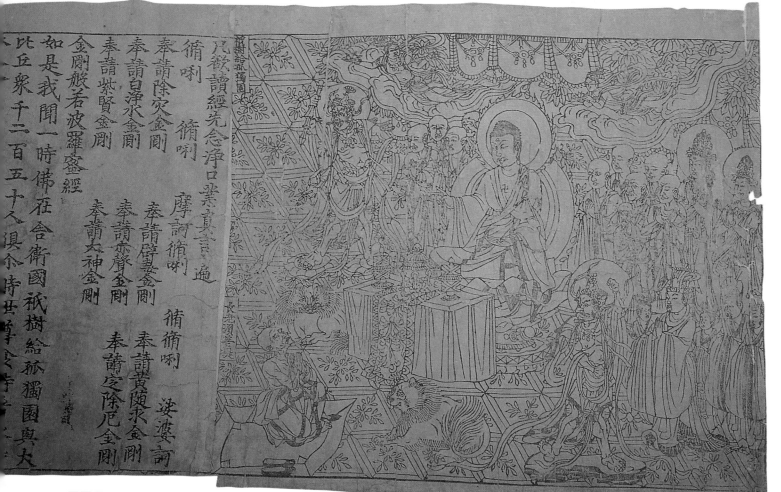

Writing was invented in the Near East so that people could keep records and accounts of their goods and transactions. Various forms of scripts were used. The earliest writing found so far is from Mesopotamia. Clay tablets with a picture script have been dated to 3200 BC. These *pictograms*, as they are called, are of fish, grain, cows, water and other things. They form lists of goods in store or for trade.

CUNEIFORM AND HIEROGLYPHIC WRITING The next form of writing is called *cuneiform* and is also found in Mesopotamia for the first time in about 2800 BC. The writing is also found on clay tablets but it is a series of wedges to form symbols which represent words.

Later on a different form of writing was developed by the Egyptians called *hieroglyphic* script. It was a sort of picture writing, too. The Egyptians eventually made up about 700 hieroglyphs.

The T'ang dynasty of China lasted from AD 618 to 906 and was a very prosperous and peaceful period in Chinese history. This period was the first to produce printed books. This one (above), which shows the Buddha addressing his disciples, was printed from a wood block on a scroll in AD 868. Before paper was invented characters were painted on to wood strips like this bamboo book (left). Strips of bamboo were tied with string and rolled into a 'book'.

Left. The names of the Buddha printed on paper found at Dunhuang dated to the 10th century AD. Right. Oracle bones have been found with inscriptions carved on them. The cracks are formed when the bone is touched by heated bronze points. The shape of the cracks gave the 'answers' of the oracle. The inscription on the right records the correct animals to be sacrificed to dead ancestors and reads 'Get ready the officers, Father second a pig, son a pig; Mother ninth a pig. . .'.

CHINESE WRITING The Chinese probably developed their own form of writing without any knowledge of writing from other civilizations. Inscriptions are known from 1500 BC onwards. There are four different sorts of script.

Pictographs are simplified pictures of objects. In *simplified pictographs*, the pictographs were slightly changed and the original pictures indicated by one or more lines. This made writing simpler and quicker.

The third and fourth types of script indicated the sound of the word as well as its idea. The last group is the most commonly found with about 9000 characters in use in AD 100. This script is still used today but now has about 60,000 characters.

ORACLE BONES A great deal of ancient Chinese writing has been found on oracle bones. These are usually the flat shoulder blades of cattle. They were used to foretell the future by observing the cracks in the bone caused by touching the bone with a metal point heated by fire.

Writing is also found on paper made from rags and cellulose and on bamboo, wood and silk. Large numbers of manuscripts have now been found during excavations of tombs.

The Art of Calligraphy

Calligraphy is the art of writing. Chinese artists and scholars used brushes and ink to draw out both words and pictures. A hard block of ink is rubbed on stone palette with water.

Ancient India
THE MAURYAN EMPIRE

Pakistan, in the north-western part of the subcontinent of India, was home to one of the world's earliest civilizations. The land around the River Indus was fertile enough to support a very large population of farmers. The river gives its name to the civilization – the Indus civilization – which developed around 2300 BC and had two main cities, Harappa and Mohenjo-Daro.

INDIAN STATES AT WAR After the cities of the Indus civilization had developed and declined, other parts of India flourished. The areas around other major rivers, like the Ganges, produced wealth from rice growing. By 600 BC there were at least 16 small states in the Ganges plain. During the fifth century BC they were at constant war with each other. The strongest took over the smaller, weaker ones and eventually they were all taken into the kingdom of Magadha.

THE MAURYAN EMPIRE ESTABLISHED The throne of the kingdom of Magadha was seized by Chandragupta Maurya at the end of the fourth century BC. He could be called the first real Emperor of India, as the Mauryan Empire which he established covered most of the subcontinent. Under his rule the Empire spread north-west

into the area around the River Indus, south into central India and even into what is now Afghanistan.

His son, Bindusara, extended the Empire again but it was Bindusara's son, Asoka, who extended the Mauryan Empire furthest.

THE EMPEROR ASOKA Asoka took over from his father in about 270 BC and reigned until his death in 232 BC. Apart from the far south, he controlled most of the subcontinent of India. It was a rich Empire; most of the population were farmers. Asoka's grandfather had established a system of governing the Empire which was actually published in a book. Asoka developed this system and there was a complicated way of collecting taxes.

TRAVEL AND TRADE Roads were an important way to control and administer the huge Empire. There was a special group of officials in the Mauryan government just for that. Major roads included the Royal Highway which ran from the capital city of Pataliputra to the north-west. The Roman Empire imported a number of goods from India. The Romans liked the cotton cloth made in India as well as the spices of southern India and its precious stones.

On the right is a representation of the Mother Goddess made out of terracotta in the first century BC. Terracotta is fired clay. Although it has elaborate decoration you can work out a face, earrings and necklaces, arms and breasts.
The Emperor Asoka became a Buddhist and was responsible for the spread of that religion. On the far right is a lime plaster figure of a Buddha, with two Buddhas on each side and two attendants behind. It is from Taxila (see page 60).

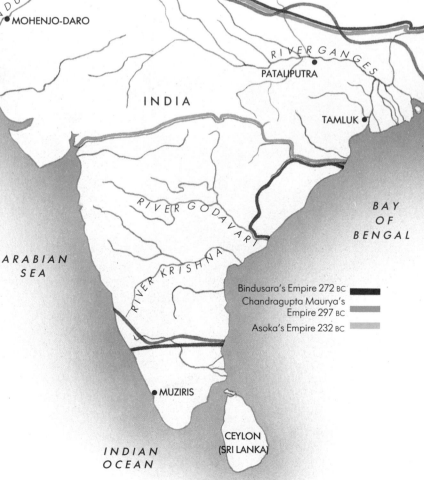

Mauryan India

India and the Romans

'The best way to sail to India is to set out from Ocelis. It's forty days' voyage to the first trading station in India called Muziris – not a desirable port of call because of the pirates in the district.' This is how the Roman writer Pliny described the most direct route across the Arabian Sea, from the entrance to the Red Sea (the port of Ocelis is now called Khawr Ghurayrah) to southern India.

TAXILA

HARAPPA

RIVER INDUS

MOHENJO-DARO

RIVER GANGES

PATALIPUTRA

INDIA

TAMLUK

RIVER GODAVARI

ARABIAN SEA

BAY OF BENGAL

RIVER KRISHNA

Bindusara's Empire 272 BC
Chandragupta Maurya's Empire 297 BC
Asoka's Empire 232 BC

MUZIRIS

CEYLON (SRI LANKA)

INDIAN OCEAN

1 The earliest people to live in the Caribbean were probably hunting and food gathering by around 5000 BC. They made tools and weapons of stone, bone and shell. From about 3000 BC various groups who knew about agriculture can be identified – mainly from their pottery and art objects. One of these groups we call the Saladoid peoples. They occupied Puerto Rico and the islands towards Trinidad and Guyana. They cultivated crops, baked bread and made pottery decorated with designs based on animals, such as tortoises and frogs.

2 Australia was probably first occupied by peoples coming from southeast Asia by sea as early as 50,000 BC. These were hunters and food gatherers. By 3000 BC people were beginning to settle and use the land for agriculture. People and ideas soon spread to the islands to the northeast. Those living in the Polynesian islands (Samoa, Tonga and the Solomon Islands, for example) spoke different languages to those in Australia or Papua New Guinea.

GOVERNING THE MAURYAN EMPIRE

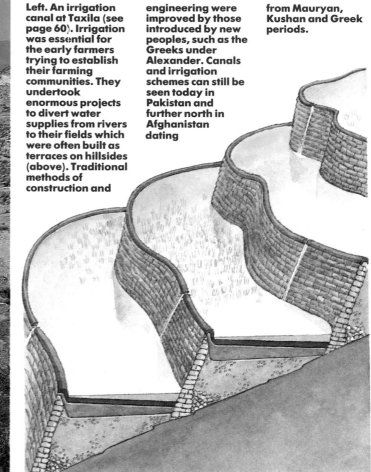

Left. An irrigation canal at Taxila (see page 60). Irrigation was essential for the early farmers trying to establish their farming communities. They undertook enormous projects to divert water supplies from rivers to their fields which were often built as terraces on hillsides (above). Traditional methods of construction and engineering were improved by those introduced by new peoples, such as the Greeks under Alexander. Canals and irrigation schemes can still be seen today in Pakistan and further north in Afghanistan dating from Mauryan, Kushan and Greek periods.

One of the signs that a civilization exists is the building of cities. The Mauryan Empire had many cities and was divided into four provinces so that the huge territory could be governed more easily. Each province had its own ruler, called a *viceroy*, appointed by the emperor. Asoka had been the viceroy of one province when his father was emperor. He ruled his province from the city of Taxila (see page 60). Asoka sent inspectors to tour the provinces every five years to check on the finances and administration.

THE ARTHASHASTRA Kautalya, who was the chief advisor to Chandragupta Maurya (see page 50), probably invented the basis of the Empire's tax system. He wrote a reference work on government called the *Arthashastra*. This work has survived and tells us a great deal about the way the government worked.

PAYING STATE TAXES The people in the cities and the farming population paid very high taxes to keep a vast standing army and a huge civil service to administer the Empire.

The two important posts in the administration were the Treasurer, who kept an account of the income from taxes, and the Chief Collector, who kept the tax records. The Chief Collector had a large number of clerks to assist him. The *Arthashastra* explains that superintendents were in charge of each department:

The Superintendent of Commerce should work out the demand or the lack of demand for various kinds of merchandise, and the rise or fall in their prices, whether the merchandise is brought by land or by water. The Superintendent will also work out the most suitable time for the merchandise to be distributed, held centrally, purchased and sold.

52

A ruined stupa, dating to about 200 BC, at Dhamekh in India. This one has ornamental stonework around it (where it has not been removed), but stupas originally developed from simple mounds.

Left. The Emperor Asoka set up very tall pillars throughout his empire. They probably marked places which were already considered sacred. Asoka used the inscriptions on these pillars and on rocks to make proclamations. Part of one inscription reads '. . . Herbs for medicine, for people and animals, where they were lacking have been imported and planted everywhere. Along the roads wells have been dug and trees planted for the enjoyment of people and animals'.

Above. Some of the decorative stonework and sculpture on stupas was very fine. These examples are from the stupa of the Jaulian monastery at Taxila (see page 60). It has now been brought inside a protective building to keep it secure. You can see that some of the stonework has already been damaged.

IN THE COUNTRYSIDE Most of the people in Mauryan India lived as farmers in small villages, growing crops and keeping animals. The land was owned by the Emperor and people paid taxes on the land, its produce and the animals. Large areas of land were cleared for agriculture, on the command of the Emperor. Frequently, people were moved by force from areas where the population was too large.

One of the most important developments during the period of the Mauryan Empire was irrigation. Reservoirs, tanks, wells and canals were all constructed. In western India one provincial governor built a dam across a river near Girnar and constructed a large lake for his region. Records show that this reservoir of water was maintained for 800 years. The Arthashastra mentions a water tax which was collected whenever the state provided help with irrigation.

TOWNS AND INDUSTRY Towns in Mauryan India were often defended. The capital of Pataliputra, near Patna, had a rampart with a huge timber frame which writers of the day said stretched for 8.4 miles along the Ganges.

The *Arthashastra* gives a record of what such a town was supposed to be like:

Royal teachers, priests, the sacrificial place, the water reservoir, and ministers shall occupy sites east by north to the palace . . . the Royal kitchen, elephant stables and the store-house shall be situated on the sides east by south . . . on the eastern side will be the merchants trading in scents, garlands, grains and liquids . . . to the west the manufacturers of worsted cloth, cotton threads, bamboo mats, skins, armour, weapons and gloves . . . either to the north or the east burial or cremation cemeteries shall be situated.

RELIGION IN THE MAURYAN EMPIRE

Buddhism

The father of Siddhartha Gautama Buddha was the ruler of the Sakya tribe in northern India (modern Nepal). There are many legends about his birth, but he seems to have been a very gifted child. At the age of 29 he received four signs which proved a turning point in his life. He saw a sick man, an old man, a corpse, and a man with a shaven head wearing a yellow robe. These signs he interpreted and called **Dukkha** (sick man) or 'suffering,' **Anicca** (old man) or 'change,' **Anatta** (corpse) or 'becoming impersonal,' and finally 'passing into a state of serenity' (shaven-headed man).

Gautama decided to leave home and search for what he called the True Wisdom. He searched for six years and finally spent the night in meditation, passing through various stages of awareness until he reached Enlightenment and became the Buddha, which can be translated as 'The Enlightened One.'

For 45 years after this he wandered around India preaching that the middle way, or **Dhamma**, between extremes was the right way for people. **Dukkha** (suffering - from the sick man). This represents the whole of a person's existence.

A wall painting from one of the caves at Ajanta. Most of the paintings illustrate events from the life of Gautama Buddha. This section shows the Buddha as a child being taught by other children.

Siddhartha Gautama Buddha was born around 566 BC in one of the small states which became part of the Mauryan Empire. He founded Buddhism, one of the world's greatest religions. He believed that each person should do good works, be disciplined in their life and meditate. After his death a group of his followers established an order of monks and began to spread this religious belief.

THE CONVERSION OF ASOKA During his reign, the Emperor Asoka became a convert to the Buddhist religion. He gave up conquering by war and lived by the new ideas of Buddhism. It became the main religion of the Empire and spread out beyond the borders, first to Sri Lanka. Buddhist monks travelled widely taking their religion to Southeast Asia, China and Japan.

The first monuments and monasteries of Buddhism were put up during the reign of Asoka. Asoka spread the word of the Buddha by inscriptions carved on pillars and flat rock surfaces all over the Empire. Asoka also built monasteries with a special central building, called a *stupa*, for the rituals. The stupa changed its shape over time. It was originally a simple mound of earth. It soon became a round stone building.

THE MONASTERY OF AJANTA In central India on the edge of the River Waghora are some of the most impressive monuments of Buddhist religion. Cut into the rock of the cliff are a number of temples and monasteries. Two temples and three monasteries were created there in the second or first centuries BC and all the rest constructed in the fifth century AD.

Below. In plan form you can see the temples and monasteries at Ajanta set in a horseshoe-shape around the River Waghora. Ajanta was an important place in the first and second centuries BC but became very important in the fifth century AD. The various religious buildings here contain some of the best Buddhist carvings and wall paintings in existence.

Above. Caves had been used for religious purposes before the Mauryan period. The caves at Ajanta were adapted by the Buddhist monks and decorated (see right) with elaborately carved columns, windows and Buddhas.

MONASTERIES OF SECOND AND FIRST CENTURIES BC

TEMPLES OF SECOND AND FIRST CENTURIES BC

TEMPLES OF FIFTH CENTURY AD

RIVER WAGHORA

TEMPLES OF FIFTH CENTURY AD

Temples were built to cover small stupas which often contained holy relics. The temples at Ajanta, in the early period, were long hall-like buildings with the stupa at one end which was half-round in shape.

Images of the Buddha and scenes from his life were usually found in temples and the wall paintings from Ajanta are some of the finest known. The first people from Europe saw them in 1819.

The buildings for the monks in the second century BC are simple in their plan. There was a central courtyard hall where the monks could gather together. Off this courtyard were the monks' individual rooms, or *cells*, with bed platforms cut out of the rock. The later monasteries were slightly more elaborate, some having two stories.

The Kushans
INVADERS FROM CHINA

The continent of India was invaded many times by foreigners who established kingdoms or even empires. The campaigns of Alexander the Great reached India; in 327 BC he conquered Gandhara, the valley of the River Kabul in present-day Afghanistan. By 325 BC he was marching home having conquered most of what is now Pakistan. The Greeks were not able to hold the region for long. The area was soon taken over by the Mauryan Emperor Chandragupta Maurya (see page 50).

NEW INVADERS IN NORTHERN INDIA The strongest, and most successful, invaders of India were a nomadic tribe from China. In the west they were known as the Tochari but their proper name seems to have been the Yueh-chih. We know of them first of all in 165 BC living near the Great Wall of China. The Yueh-chih tribe was defeated by its neighbors and was forced to move west and settle in the region where the present-day countries of India, Pakistan, China, Afghanistan and the territory of the former USSR meet.

THE KUSHANS One part of the tribe of the Yueh-chih took over control and eventually established a very large empire. Their Chinese name was Kuei-shang which became known as Kushan. The Kushan Empire was established around AD 60. The greatest of the rulers was Kanishka I who began ruling in about AD 78, although we are not certain about dates at this time.

THE EMPIRE OF THE KUSHANS The Kushans eventually established an empire which stretched from the River Ganges in the east to the Caspian Sea in the west, from the River Jaxartes which flows into the Aral Sea in the north to the mouth of the Indus Valley in the south. To their west was the Empire of the Parthians (see page 62). Further west were the Romans. The Kushans were in a good position to trade with the Romans and their territory lay on the 'Silk Road' between Rome and China.

CITIES OF THE KUSHANS Kanishka I made the capital of his Empire the city of Purushapura close to the Hindu Kush mountain range north of the River Indus. The second most important city of the Empire was at Mathura, further east on the River Jumna.

Kushan rulers took grand titles for themselves which they borrowed from the Persians and the Chinese. The

Kushan Empire in AD 150

The Kushan Empire of the ruler Kanishka I was situated in a key position between the states of India and the Parthian Empire. This position gave them access for trade with the Roman world.

Left. The reverse, or back, of a silver coin of Ardashir I who took over the Parthian Empire in about AD 224 (see page 62). He attacked neighboring peoples, including the Kushans. The coin shows a fire altar.

most usual were *Maharajatiraja* meaning King of Kings and *Daivaputra* meaning Son of Heaven. One ruler called himself *Kaisura* – Caesar – obviously wishing to be as powerful as a Roman emperor.

THE END OF THE KUSHAN EMPIRE The great Kushan Empire lasted from the middle of the first century to the third century AD. The Empire was invaded by the Persians and almost destroyed. In the fourth century a new ruler revived it but by the following century the region had been taken over completely by new foreign invaders – the Huns – coming from the north.

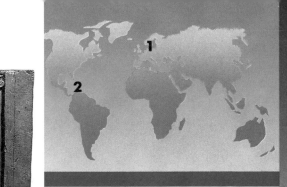

A group of gods of the sea from northern India in Gandharan style. These carvings of the Kushan period show the influence of Greek and Roman art.

1 The year AD 60 was a significant date in the history of the Romans in Britain. The tribes in the east of Britain considered themselves hard pressed during the winter when the Roman tax collectors demanded payment. The fierce queen of the Iceni tribe, called Boudica, rose up against the Romans. She led an army of 100,000 through East Anglia and destroyed the towns of Colchester, Verulamium (now St Albans) and London. She went on to annihilate a Roman legion which was sent against her. She was stopped eventually and Roman order imposed again.

2 The city of Teotihuacan developed over a period of 600 years. By AD 500 it was the sixth largest city in the world with a population of about 200,000. The city was laid out on a grid system and covered over 8 square miles. The people believed this was the birthplace of the Sun and the Moon gods. There is a square dedicated to the Moon and the famous Pyramid of the Sun.

BLACK SEA

CASPIAN SEA

ALEXANDRESCHATA

MEDITERRANEAN SEA

ALEXANDRIA

JERUSALEM

BABYLON

PERSEPOLIS

ALEXANDRIA AREION

PERSIAN GULF

RED SEA

ARABIAN SEA

Alexander's Empire

Greek influences appeared in India because of the invasion of the Greek ruler Alexander the Great (see also page 62). The map shows his invasion route and the empire he established to the borders of the Mauryan kingdom. Notice how many of the names of towns begin with or are called Alexandria – Alexander's town.

☐ Extent of Alexander's Empire

⟶ Alexander's route

This sculpture in relief in the Gandharan style of the third century AD shows a group of ascetics. These were followers of religion who denied themselves any luxuries and lived an extremely simple and austere life.

ART IN THE KUSHAN EMPIRE

During the period of the Kushan Empire artists and architects working in different materials produced some fine work. Art was influenced by contacts with Greece because of the invasions of Alexander the Great. Bronze sculptures and plaster-work were imported into the Kushan Empire from Alexandria. The Buddhist religion provided plenty of scenes and saints as subjects for art. Art in northern India became a combination of Indian and Greek ideas and styles and is known as Graeco-Indian or Graeco-Buddhist art.

GANDHARA ART The art of this period is usually known as Gandharan art, named after the area in the northern part of the Kushan Empire. The Buddha himself (see page 54) was represented in sculpture rather like a Greek mother-figure. Indian artists also modelled the Buddha on the Greek god Apollo.

There were sculptures in stone but also in fired clay, or *terracotta*, for those who could not afford expensive stone. Little terracotta figures were used as toys and as decoration in the home. A form of decorative molded plasterwork, called *stucco*, was introduced from Alexander's Empire and used to decorate Kushan monasteries throughout the East.

This is part of a free-standing gate to the Great Stupa at Sanchi in central India. It was built in about the first century BC. It is covered with elaborate sculpture and carving in a realistic style showing Buddhist legends. At the bottom right is a female native spirit, called a *yaksi*, which guarded treasures. The spirals suggest the rolled ends of scrolls on which stories were written.

Left. A sculpture of the Buddha, as the 'Enlightened One,' in the Gandharan style from the second or third centuries AD.

Below. A carved relief showed Gautama Buddha (see page 54) as he grew up. In it, he is travelling in a chariot pulled by two rams. Gautama is going to his lessons with his schoolmates who are carrying writing boards and ink pots.

Above and right. The female was a favorite subject in Indian art. Both these objects are from Mathura near Delhi. Artists from Mathura developed a lively form of art and introduced the first images of the Buddha. These objects are both from around 150 BC. You can see (above) a terracotta which decorated a building and (right) the figure of a woman, also in terracotta.

THE CITY OF TAXILA

The excavated ruins of the cities at Taxila are now open to visitors.

The ancient city of Taxila is in modern Pakistan north-west of Rawalpindi. The location of Taxila meant that it was an important trading city for nearly 1000 years. Major trading routes passed through Taxila and its merchants traded not only between the Romans and India but also provided goods from China.

Taxila began to be prosperous in the sixth century BC when it was part of the Persian Empire. The Persians built the first roads there to govern their empire and for trade. By Alexander the Great's time Taxila was an independent kingdom. We know that Alexander the Great visited the city in 326 BC.

THE THREE CITIES At three different times cities were built at Taxila. The first is called the Bhir Mound and must have been the one which Alexander the Great visited. This was the site of the original Persian city. It was part of the territory conquered by the first Mauryan

emperor, Chandragupta Maurya. The city of the Mauryan period lies over the Persian one. The city has not been fully excavated but some of the narrow main streets lined with houses and shops have been uncovered.

SIRKAP After the Mauryan Empire Taxila was conquered, around 189 BC, by Greeks who had settled in Bactria (now northeast Afghanistan). A Greek city was laid out across the river from the original settlement at a place known as Sirkap.

Sirkap was laid out like new Greek cities in other countries with straight streets cutting across each other at right angles. Houses and shops were built inside the rectangular blocks which the streets created. Also typical of a Greek city was a high point called an *acropolis* enclosed by a wall. The most famous acropolis is the one in Athens, capital of ancient and modern Greece. The

The Location of Taxila

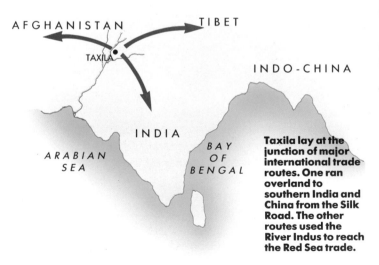

Taxila lay at the junction of major international trade routes. One ran overland to southern India and China from the Silk Road. The other routes used the River Indus to reach the Red Sea trade.

There were a number of stupas and monasteries at Taxila both inside the city and around it. The sculpture above comes from a monastery there. The plan on the left shows the location of the three cities at Taxila. Excavations to uncover the city began in the 1920s but later archaeological work has shown how extensive the settlement was and how complex was its history.

whole city was surrounded and defended by a wall. Outside the city walls, at Jundial, the Greeks built a great temple.

The defenses of Sirkap were not enough to stop it from being attacked, and taken, by a nomadic tribe called the Shaka in the early first century BC and then again by the Parthians around AD 19. Both peoples occupied Sirkap.

SIRSUKH The final settlers at Taxila were the Kushans

in the mid first century AD. They occupied Sirkap at first but then built a new city at Sirsukh. It was built like the cities in the country they had originally come from. Its shape, marked out by a wall for defense, was a parallelogram – that is, a rectangle where the opposite sides are parallel but the corners do not form right angles.

Around the three cities were a number of stupas and temples built by the Mauryan and Kushan peoples.

The Parthian and Sassanian Empires
SHAPUR I AND THE DEFEAT OF ROME

Two peoples, the Medes and the Persians, came from central Asia into what is now Iran. The Persians became the controllers of the land after their King Cyrus defeated the king of the Medes in 550 BC. The Persian Empire grew to cover a vast area stretching from northern Greece to North Africa and east to India. Under two of their emperors, Darius and Xerxes, they tried to conquer Greece. Darius was defeated at the famous

Part of the column put up in Rome by the Emperor Trajan to celebrate his victory over the Dacians in AD 114.

battle of Marathon in 490 BC and Xerxes at the Battle of Salamis in 480 BC.

ALEXANDER THE GREAT The great Persian Empire came to an end much later in 331 BC. Alexander, a ruler from Macedon in northern Greece who became known as Alexander the Great, marched right through Persian territory to its easternmost limits – the River Indus in Pakistan.

THE PARTHIANS After Alexander's Empire had broken up at his death, various peoples and rulers took parts for themselves. Among these were the Parthians. They were originally a nomadic people from the eastern side of the Caspian Sea. They gradually took over more and more territory and established their own empire which was partly eastern and partly Greek. The Parthians were noted for their skill with horses and as cavalry fighters.

The limits of their Empire in the west touched the Roman Empire. At first they were unconquered by the Romans who were forced to negotiate with them. Under the Roman Emperor Trajan in AD 114 some of their territory was taken over.

THE SASSANIANS The Parthian Empire was finally taken over in the third century AD by the people who came to be known as the Sassanians. From one part of the Parthian Empire on the Persian Gulf, Persis, Sassanian princes built a new empire.

The first, called Prince Ardashir, led a revolt against Parthian rule and killed the last Parthian king, Artabanus V, in about AD 224. From then on Ardashir attacked the other peoples around, including the Romans and the Kushans.

His son, Shapur I, conquered most of the territory of the Kushan Empire and defeated three Roman emperors. Gordian III was killed in battle, Philip was forced to make peace with him and he captured and executed the Emperor Valerian in about AD 260. He shamed the Romans by forcing Roman prisoners of war to resettle in a new city which he called Veh-Antiok-Shapur, which means 'The city of Shapur, better than Antioch.' Antioch was the Roman capital city of the province of Syria.

The Parthian and Sassanian Empires

Parthian Empire
Sassanian Empire

MACEDONIA

MEDITERRANEAN SEA

CASPIAN SEA

BABYLON

SUSA

PERSEPOLIS

EGYPT

RED SEA

INDIA

ARABIAN SEA

1 After the collapse of the Han Dynasty in China in AD 220, the country broke into small states which were often at war with each other. For 45 years there were three states. Then the power shifted to two states — the Northern Wei and the Ch'i state in the south. China was not reunited as a country again until the first Sui Emperor came to power in AD 581.

2 Some 2,400 miles from the coast of Chile lies Rapanui, or Easter Island — famous for its gigantic statues 10 to 33 ft high. The name of the island comes from a Dutch navigator, Jacob Roggeveen, who was the first European to visit it on Easter Day in 1722. The island remained uninhabited until about AD 500 when Polynesians settled there. They took plants with them and cultivated the banana, palm, taro and yam. The statues found there, called *moai*, are images cut into volcanic rock of the head and the top half of the body.

Left. A rock carving at Naqsh-i Rustam near Persepolis. It shows the king, Shapur I, on horseback towering over two Romans. They are the Roman emperors Philip (shown kneeling) and Valerian (standing). They are both paying homage to Shapur.

Above. This silver-gilt dish, now in the Hermitage Museum in Leningrad in Russia, shows the Sassanian king, Ardashir III who reigned from AD 628 to AD 630. You can see the king is hunting from horseback.

THE ART OF THE SASSANIAN EMPIRE

Far left. A fine example of gold craft showing a Sassanian king in relief.
Top. An eagle made from glass crystal.
Below. Bronze figure of a monster dated to the seventh/eighth century AD. Creatures like this dragon are often found in the art of the Sassanian period.

Ardashir was known as *shahanshah* which means 'king of kings.' The government of the Sassanian Empire was established in a very formal way; serving below the King of Kings were various 'grades' of officials and peoples. There were nobles, priests, warriors, civil servants and farming peoples. The religion, called Zoroastrianism, founded by the Persian prophet Zoroaster, became the official state religion.

CHINA AND THE SASSANIANS The links between the Sassanian Empire and China were very close. There was a great deal of trade between the two peoples along the Silk Road. China imported works of art in gold, glass, crystals and textiles. Chinese art was influenced by what they imported from the west. Chinese work in gold was begun during this period and goldsmiths from the Sassanian Empire must have travelled to China to work. Archaeologists have found more than 1200 Sassanid coins in China, most of them from Xinjiang.

SASSANIAN ART The Sassanian period is particularly noted for its fine works of art, often in precious metals and stones. Molding in glass became an art form and gemstones were cut into shapes. Cups, bowls and dishes of silver were made with people – especially kings – animals and plants shown in *relief*, where the figures stand out from the background. Examples of the different art forms are shown here.

Left. This relief sculpture is carved out of brick on the wall of a temple. Some features have also been enamelled. It pictures Ahuramazda, the god of gods, at the top. Ahuramazda was often shown giving the right of ruling to the Sassanian kings. Ahuramazda is shown as having a dish-shaped body with large symmetrical wings and the vertical tail of a bird. He hovers in the heavens above the earth. Below the god are two winged sphinxes.

Below. A very fine example of Sassanian artistry in silver. This horse's head shows every detail of the harness with its decorated trappings.

Left. This cameo shows the Sassanian King Shapur I (see page 62) capturing the Roman Emperor Valerian. This victory over the Romans, and Shapur's defeat of Gordian and Philip, were often the subject for sculpture and decoration on a variety of objects.

65

THE PEOPLE OF THE NOK CULTURE

In Europe people had discovered how to use stone, then copper and bronze and finally iron to make tools and weapons. In Africa, south of the Sahara, the period when stone was used was followed by an iron age. Iron was used for most tools and was introduced by two very different routes. The River Nile was the first route by which the idea of using iron traveled from Egypt, in about 500 BC, to the Kingdom of Meroë. In about 450 BC iron-working came from the Carthaginian cities of North Africa to where the Rivers Niger and Benue meet in the land now called Nigeria. The earliest furnaces for smelting iron ore in Nigeria are at Taruga.

In this area one particular way of life has been identified and called the Nok Culture. It lasted from the eighth century BC until the second century AD.

The people living in the region around the Rivers Niger and Benue were farmers. By about 1000 BC they had been gathering food, hunting and fishing and had begun to produce food by farming as well. Cattle, sheep and goats were all introduced to the area from elsewhere. We know about these animals not only from bones found on archaeological excavations but from rock paintings and figurines. Crops like sorghum and millet, which were found wild, were also grown.

The people of the Nok Culture were discovered in the middle of this century when a large number of their works of art turned up in tin mining operations. Little is known about their villages or towns. Only one has been properly excavated at Samun Dukiya in the Nok Valley. This site was occupied in the third century BC. No houses had survived but plenty of objects – arrow and spear heads, bracelets, pounding and grinding stones for food, fired-clay pots as well as animal bones – were found.

Religious shrines were set up on the edges of land which was cultivated. The shrines were usually washed away each year as the rivers flooded. In fact, as these iron-working people cut more and more trees down for the furnaces, so land was eroded and washed away.

THE ART OF THE NOK These people of Nok are now best known for their art which tells us so much about the way people looked then. Their art came in the form of terracotta figurines – some lifesize. Usually only the heads have survived. Some figurines are of monkeys, elephants and snakes.

Typical of the art of the Nok is this human head made from terracotta. It must once have been part of a complete figure. The features of the face are carefully modelled and also exaggerated. Two holes in the eyes indicate the pupils. The hair is shown in a tightly arranged style. Some Nok heads indicate diseases or deformities; one is made to show a cataract in one eye and paralysis of the face.

It is thought that the Nok heads and figurines were used in some ritual or religious way. This one (above) is of a kneeling man. Figurines are often shown with the head out of proportion to the body. Animals were also a favorite subject for terracottas as this elephant (left) shows. The artist has taken care to mold the detail of its features.

1 Hunters were living in the Arctic since the end of the last Ice Age. Groups moved across the land bridge in the Bering Sea in about 10,000 BC. These Inuit (or Eskimo) were found all around the Arctic Ocean from Greenland to Siberia. The Inuit made stone tools and used them to make both weapons and tools out of bone and also to carve objects. At the same time in Lappland a people called the Saami were living as hunters and fishers.

2 From about 300 BC to AD 300 the Yayoi spread from the Kyushu area of southern Japan to Honshu in the north. The people of the Yayoi were rice farmers. They also grew crops such as wheat, barley and melons and hunted and fished. They built a variety of houses — some partly below ground, others on stilts — in small settlements. The coastal fishing people, called the Jomon, resisted this settled agricultural way of life at first but had adopted it by about AD 300.

Ironworking in Ancient Africa

To make objects out of iron it is necessary to melt down iron ore at a high temperature. Iron ore is not pure iron but a mixture of iron and another material such as silicates. 'Smelting' the ore removes everything except the iron. A temperature of 1150°C or 2102°F is needed to make the waste, called 'slag,' run off.

Various types of furnaces survive which were used to smelt iron ore. The simplest is just a hollowed out space in the ground lined with clay. The iron ore is placed in layers interleaved with charcoal. Bellows help firing.

It is more efficient to smelt the iron ore in a 'reducing' atmosphere and so more complex furnaces were invented. This type of furnace has a clay cover with an built-in draught which makes the process more efficient. Two types of furnaces are shown here. On the left a clay dome is built over the hollow. The one on the right has a funnel-shaped cover. Both produce a draught aided by bellows inserted into the dome or funnel by means of a fired clay pipe called a tuyere.

The idea of using iron for tools and weapons spread down from the northern coasts of Africa to the area where the people of the Nok culture lived. The knowledge was probably brought south by the nomadic Berbers who learned about ironworking from the Carthaginians.

Charcoal is needed to produce iron. The nomadic Berbers in northern Africa may have traded their goods with the Nok people for charcoal, and introduced ironworking that way.

Iron routes

Area of the Nok culture

AXUM: ANCIENT KINGDOM OF ETHIOPIA

The Kingdom of Axum played an important part in the trade with Rome and with the Kushan Empire of India (see page 56) and lasted from around AD 100 to AD 1000. It was the center of a network of trade routes.

The name, Axum, is first recorded in a guide for seafarers and traders written at the end of the first century AD. The author of the *Periplus Maris Erythraei*, which means 'Circumnavigation of the Erythrean Sea,' was an Egyptian merchant.

THE PORT OF ADULIS The *Periplus* mentions the port of the Kingdom of Axum:

Adulis is a large village three days' journey from Koloe, a town in the interior of the country and the chief market for ivory. From Koloe to the city of the Axumites, Axum, is another five days' journey. Here is brought all the ivory from the land beyond the Nile and from here it is taken to Adulis.

THE IMPORT AND EXPORT TRADE IN AXUM The Kingdom of Axum, in Ethiopia on the coast of the Red Sea, was not only in an excellent position to trade with the Roman world, Arabia and India but it also had a variety of goods and produce which people wanted. The most important export was ivory from elephants' tusks used to carve luxury items. The other exports included slaves, gold, rhinoceros horn, hippopotamus teeth and hides, monkeys and other live animals, obsidian, emeralds, tortoise shell and spices.

The Axumites imported iron, objects of precious metals, glass ointment jars from Egypt, Roman amphorae (wine and oil containers), clothes and textiles, sugarcane, vegetable oil and spices.

THE PEOPLE OF AXUM Most of the population of Axum were farmers. They grew wheat and other cereal crops and kept herds of cattle, sheep and goats. They also had mules and asses. They hunted elephants for their tusks but also captured and trained them for their kings to use. Many were skilled in crafts such as metal working and pottery or trades such as building.

The people were ruled by a King of Kings in Axum itself. Minor kings in charge of the smaller kingdoms around were subject to him and had to pay a yearly tax or tribute – collected from the people. The King of Axum would often collect this tribute in person.

Tall, thin standing stones, called *stelae*, are a feature of Axum. This one is carved from a single block of granite and is over 69 feet high. Stelae were carved to represent multi-story buildings and stand over underground tombs.

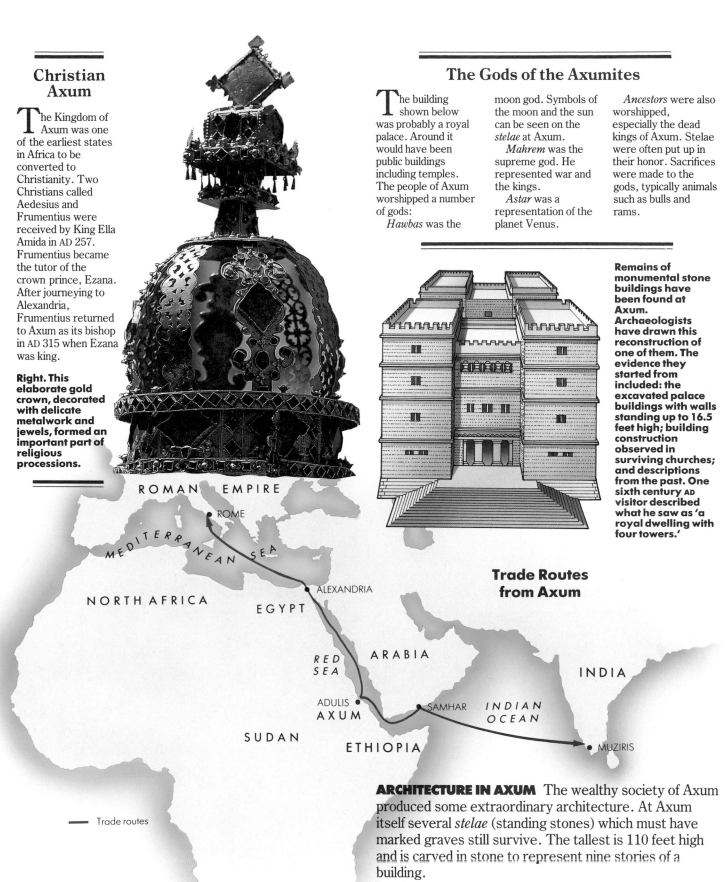

Christian Axum

The Kingdom of Axum was one of the earliest states in Africa to be converted to Christianity. Two Christians called Aedesius and Frumentius were received by King Ella Amida in AD 257. Frumentius became the tutor of the crown prince, Ezana. After journeying to Alexandria, Frumentius returned to Axum as its bishop in AD 315 when Ezana was king.

Right. This elaborate gold crown, decorated with delicate metalwork and jewels, formed an important part of religious processions.

The Gods of the Axumites

The building shown below was probably a royal palace. Around it would have been public buildings including temples. The people of Axum worshipped a number of gods:

Hawbas was the moon god. Symbols of the moon and the sun can be seen on the *stelae* at Axum.

Mahrem was the supreme god. He represented war and the kings.

Astar was a representation of the planet Venus.

Ancestors were also worshipped, especially the dead kings of Axum. Stelae were often put up in their honor. Sacrifices were made to the gods, typically animals such as bulls and rams.

Remains of monumental stone buildings have been found at Axum. Archaeologists have drawn this reconstruction of one of them. The evidence they started from included: the excavated palace buildings with walls standing up to 16.5 feet high; building construction observed in surviving churches; and descriptions from the past. One sixth century AD visitor described what he saw as 'a royal dwelling with four towers.'

Trade Routes from Axum

ROMAN EMPIRE
ROME
MEDITERRANEAN SEA
NORTH AFRICA
EGYPT
ALEXANDRIA
ARABIA
RED SEA
INDIA
ADULIS
AXUM
SAMHAR
INDIAN OCEAN
SUDAN
ETHIOPIA
MUZIRIS

— Trade routes

ARCHITECTURE IN AXUM The wealthy society of Axum produced some extraordinary architecture. At Axum itself several *stelae* (standing stones) which must have marked graves still survive. The tallest is 110 feet high and is carved in stone to represent nine stories of a building.

Several elaborate buildings have been excavated and recorded at Axum. They show a number of rooms grouped around various courtyards, all within the same building. The skilful builders of Axum used both stone and timber in construction.

PETRA: CAPITAL OF THE NABATEANS

The peoples who lived on the eastern edges of the Roman Empire were in a good position to trade their own goods and produce. They also acted as merchants providing goods from further away for the Romans. This was especially true of the people called the Nabateans in southern Arabia.

THE NABATEANS The Nabateans were nomadic people who drove herds of animals and traded goods. They took the land south of Jerusalem from the Edomite tribe in the fourth century BC and began to settle in the valleys.

The Nabateans grew rich and powerful from their trade. They were on the most important routes from India, the Red Sea, Egypt and Europe. They were in a position to control this trade and to impose taxes on traders who passed through their lands. They invented a special saddle for camels and became skilled in camel-back fighting.

FRANKINCENSE AND MYRRH The incense states or kingdoms along the Red Sea grew produce which could not be obtained anywhere else. Frankincense and myrrh were among the gifts offered to the child Christ and were in demand in the ancient world long before Christ's time.

Frankincense is the gum resin from a tree grown around the Red Sea and was used to burn as incense in religious ceremonies. It produces a pleasant smell when burnt. It was also used for *embalming* or preserving bodies. The Egyptians, living on the western side of the Red Sea, bought large quantities of frankincense.

Myrrh is similar to frankincense. It is also a gum resin from a tree and was also used for incense and embalming. Myrrh was also used in making perfumes and cosmetics.

Frankincense and myrrh trees were grown in large numbers in these incense states. Fields were created and irrigation systems constructed.

Nabatea and the Areas of Incense Cultivation

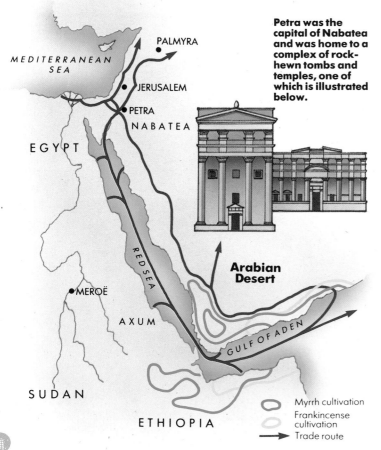

Petra was the capital of Nabatea and was home to a complex of rock-hewn tombs and temples, one of which is illustrated below.

MEDITERRANEAN SEA

PALMYRA

JERUSALEM

PETRA

NABATEA

EGYPT

RED SEA

MEROË

AXUM

Arabian Desert

GULF OF ADEN

SUDAN

ETHIOPIA

◯ Myrrh cultivation
◯ Frankincense cultivation
→ Trade route

Opposite left. This is the Khasneh, or Treasury, built in the first century BC. Local people believed the treasure was in the urn 132 feet above ground and peppered the monument with gunshots.

Above. The rock-cut royal tombs at Petra on the cliff face of the Esh Shara mountains. Many tombs were elaborately carved.

Right. The largest rock-cut monument at Petra is called El Deir – 'The Monastery' – but is in fact an elaborate tomb built in the first century AD. The doorway measures 26.4 feet high, and leads to a large inner chamber.

PETRA The city of Petra was the capital of the kingdoms of the Edomites and the Nabateans. Its wealth came from its unique position on major trade routes. In the desert, but with a good water supply, the city lay in a valley between mountain ranges. It must have been a trading center as early as the fifth century BC, but was most prosperous between 100 BC and AD 150.

The Nabateans traded with the Romans but eventually were taken over by them. The Roman general Pompey campaigned against them in 63 BC but they did not finally lose their independence until AD 106 when the Emperor Trajan made their territory the province of Arabia.

The city is famous today for its fine buildings in the middle of the desert. It was called the 'rose red city' because of the color of the stone. It has about 4000 tombs carved into the rock cliffs which surround the city.

The World Beyond the Roman Empire
TIME CHART

	CHINA	MAURYAN KINGDOM/ KUSHAN EMPIRE	PARTHIAN AND SASSANIAN EMPIRES	AFRICA
BC				
800		Rise of cities and states in Ganges Valley		Beginnings of Nok culture
600		16 states established. Elephants used in war.		Nubian capital moves to Meroë
566		Birth of Siddhartha Gautama, founder of Buddhism		
500	Cast iron first used. First coinage.			
450				Iron-working from Carthage to Nigeria
403	Inter-state wars			
350	Crossbow invented			
331			Persian Empire comes to an end	
327		Alexander the Great in India		
321		Chandragupta founds Mauryan Empire		
270		Asoka takes over Mauryan throne		
240			Parthian Dynasty begins in northern Persia	
232		Asoka dies		
221	China unified under Ch'in Shi-huang-ti			
210	Emperor Ch'in buried			
206	Han Dynasty begins			
146				Rome destroys Carthage. West coast explored.
115			Parthia controls Persia	
53			Parthia stems Roman expansion east	
AD				
50				Kingdom of Axum develops
60		Kushan Empire established		
105	First paper used			
106				Nabatean lands made a Roman province
114>6			Trajan's war with Parthians	
150	Buddhism reaches China			
200	Rise of small states. Han Dynasty threatened.			
220	Han Dynasty comes to an end			
240		Empire taken over by Shapur I		
260			Roman Emperor Valerian captured by Shapur I	
320		Founding of Gupta dynasty. Kushan Empire reestablished		
325				Axum destroys kingdom of Meroë
429				Vandals invade N. Africa
500		Decline of Gupta dynasty. Huns take over Kushan Empire.		
641				Arabs conquer Egypt and invade N. Africa
642			Sassanian Empire taken over by Arabs	

acropolis   The highest point in a Greek town, usually defended. The Acropolis in Athens is the most famous, with the temple called the Parthenon dedicated to the city's patron goddess, Athena.

aediles   Four elected officials of the Roman government in charge of public works and state records.

amphitheater   Translates as "theater in the round" because of its oval shape. Used for gladiatorial and animal fights.

amphorae   Huge pottery jars used to transport and store wine, olive oil and fish sauce.

Aqua Appia   First aqueduct to be built in Rome to carry water supplies into the city in 312 BC. Named after the politician who had it built, Appius Claudius.

aqueducts   Overground water channels often raised on arches over rivers, ravines or buildings.

barbarians   The name used by the Romans for anyone who was not Roman or did not speak Latin.

basilicas   Large aisled buildings in Roman town centers for law courts and public ceremonies.

canabae   Civilian settlement which grew up outside a Roman fort providing shops and other services for soldiers.

cavalry   Mounted unit of an army.

cells   Small rooms inhabited by priests or monks.

censors   Elected officials who kept a register of all Roman citizens.

circus   Stadium used for Roman chariot racing.

colonies   Towns set up for retired Roman soldiers and their families in the provinces.

consul   The highest political office in Roman government. Each year two consuls were in charge of the army, the civilian government and the law courts.

corpus vigilum   Roman army units which provided police protection and a fire service for towns.

cuneiform   Early form of writing invented by the Sumerians and made from wedge shapes pressed into clay.

curator aquarum   Superintendent of the aqueducts and water supply appointed for Roman towns.

cursus publicus   Official courier service set up by the Roman Emperor Augustus.

Daivaputra   Indian title used by the Kushans to mean "Son of Heaven."

dictator   Appointed by the Roman consuls in serious emergency. Held absolute power for six months.

dioceses   Twelve districts set up by the Roman Emperor Diocletian to govern the Empire.

dynasty   Family who rules a country or empire, passing power on from generation to generation.

embalming   Method of drying and preserving a dead body. Egyptian mummies are the best known of embalmed bodies.

eques singularis   Member of the Roman Emperor's mounted bodyguard.

equites   Class of Roman citizens who owned property. Originally called equites, or knights, because they were rich enough to provide a horse and armor in war.

evidence   Material, written or physical remains, which give clues to the story of the past. Collected by archaeologists and historians.

forum   Originally the open market area of a Roman town. Most public buildings (law courts, government offices and temples) were grouped around the forum.

gladiators   Professional fighters in the amphitheater who usually fought to the death against each other or animals.

grammaticus   Teacher of Roman children from about 12 years of age. He taught literature, history, math and astronomy.

hieroglyphic   Form of writing using drawings to indicate words, syllables or letters. Used by the ancient Egyptians.

lacquerwork   Form of art used by the ancient Chinese. Objects of wood were coated with a shiny lacquer which brought out the colors and gave it a sheen.

legio   Roman legion, the main unit of the army, usually made up of about 5500 men.

limes   Permanent defended barrier built by the Romans at an edge of their Empire. One limes stretched between the Rivers Rhine and Danube.

magister equitum   Second-in-command to a Roman dictator. He was in charge of the cavalry.

magister ludi   Teacher of reading, writing and arithmetic to Roman children aged seven to 12.

Magna Graecia   Literally "Great Greece," was land in southern Italy and Sicily settled by the Greeks.

Maharjatiraja   Indian title used by the Kushans meaning King of Kings.

manes   Originally the word for the souls of dead Romans. Came to mean the gods of the dead.

mimus   Short sketch about city life performed in a Roman theater.

mosaic   Floor or wall decoration made up of many very small fragments (called *tesserae*) of stone, tile or glass. Complicated patterns and pictures could be made in mosaic form.

official   Someone appointed or elected to carry out a specific job, such as a Roman aedile.

optimates   Political party in late republican Rome made up of wealthy men.

opus sectile   Type of Roman marble flooring. Small pieces of marble made up patterns or pictures. The pieces of marble were larger than in mosaic floors.

pantomimus   Ballet with music; usually about legends of the Roman past, performed in the theater.

patricians Wealthy land-owning people who could trace their origins back to early Roman times — the nobles.

Periplus Maris Erythraei Guide for seafarers and merchants written by an Egyptian merchant in the first century AD.

pictograms Earliest form of writing invented in Mesopotamia which used pictures to indicate objects, animals, people and nature.

pictographs Early form of Chinese writing using simplified pictures of objects.

plebeians Name given to the ordinary working people of Roman society.

pontifex Roman priest who carried out ceremonies and sacrifices for the gods.

populares Political party in late republican Rome made up of people who wanted reforms for ordinary working people.

praetors Officials elected as judges of the Roman state.

provinces Lands conquered or taken over by the Romans outside Italy. Provinces were part of the Roman Empire.

quaestors Officials elected to look after the finances of the Roman state.

rampart Bank, usually of earth strengthened with wood or stone, around a fort or town.

relief Form of carving or molding where the forms stand out from the background.

respublica The word the Romans used for their democratic state — our word republic.

rex King — a word hated by the Romans who threw out their kings and established a republican form of government.

Rhus Verniciflua Tree growing in the Far East which produces lacquer.

senate Group of ex-officials of the Roman state who formed a type of "parliament" to discuss and debate government business.

shahanshah Title of Ardashir, the Sassanian king, meaning King of Kings.

silphium A vegetable, now extinct.

simplified pictographs Form of Chinese writing where pictographs were changed from pictures to one or more lines.

stelae Standing pillars with inscriptions cut on them.

stucco Form of plasterwork used to produce moldings or picture decorations on walls and ceilings.

stupa Round building (originally a mound of earth) in the center of Buddhist monasteries used for rituals.

terracotta Kiln-fired pottery molding used mostly for decoration on buildings and statues.

theater Place where plays were performed. Roman theaters were D-shaped, the audience sitting in the arched section.

tribunes Elected by the Roman plebeian class to look after their interests in government.

tribuni militum Officers in the Roman legion who recruited the soldiers and served the legionary commander.

vallus Roman harvesting machine for wheat pushed into the crop by a horse or donkey.

vicarius Governor of a diocese, or district, appointed by the Roman Emperor Diocletian.

viceroy Governor of a district appointed by the Mauryan emperor.

vilica Housekeeper of a Roman country estate.

vilicus Roman farm manager.

villa Roman term for a house in the country or by the sea, or a country estate.

villa urbana House of the owner of a Roman country estate.

villa fructuaria Buildings on a Roman farm for storage of animals or produce.

villa rustica House where the manager of a Roman farm lived.

villa urbana House of the owner of a Roman country estate.

INDEX

Further Reading

GENERAL REFERENCE

*Encyclopedia of Ancient
    Civilizations* by Arthur
    Cotterell (Viking Penguin,
    1989)
Atlas of Ancient History by
    Colin McEvedy (Viking
    Pengiun, 1986)
*Mummies, Masks, and
    Mourners* by Margaret
    Berrill (Dutton, 1990)
Secret Cities by Mike
    Corbishley (Dutton, 1989)
Secrets From the Past by
    Gene S. Stuart (National
    Geographic, 1979)

ROME

*Ancient Rome: A Cultural
    Atlas for Young People* by
    Mike Corbishley (Facts On
    File, 1989)
*What Do We Know About the
    Romans?* by Mike
    Corbishley (Facts On File,
    1992)
Rome by Simon James
    (Watts, Franklin, 1987)
*City: A Story of Roman
    Planning and Construction*
    by David Macaulay
    (Houghton Mifflin, 1983)
The Roman Army by Peter
    Hodge (Longman, 1977)
Roman Army by J. Wilkes
    (Cambridge U., 1973)

Picture Acknowledgements

The author and publishers would like to acknowledge, with thanks, the following photographic sources:

Front cover (left) Ronald Sheridan, (right) Ancient Art & Architecture Collection; p.10 (upper) Archiv für Kunst und Geschichte (AKG), (lower) AKG; p.11 (left) AKG, (right) Michael Holford; p.12 C. M. Dixon; p.15 Ancient Art & Architecture Collection; p.17 (left) M. Corbishley, (right) Michael Holford; p.19 Mansell Collection; p.21 (all photographs) Ancient Art & Architecture Collection; p.22 Michael Holford; p.23 (left and right) AKG; p.24 C.M. Dixon; p.26 C.M. Dixon; p.27 (left) Trustees of the British Museum, (upper centre) Judges Postcards Ltd, Hastings, (right) Tyne & Wear Museums, (centre) Werner Forman Archive; p.28 (upper and lower) C.M. Dixon; p.30 C.M. Dixon, p.31 Michael Holford; p.33 (upper and lower) C.M. Dixon; p.34 (left) Michael Holford, (centre and right) Sonia Halliday Photographs; p.35 Trustees of the British Museum; p.36 C.M. Dixon; p.39 (left and upper) C.M. Dixon, (centre) Ancient Art & Architecture Collection, (right) Werner Forman Archive; p.42 Robert Harding Picture Library; p.43 MacQuitty Collection; p.44 (upper) Robert Harding Picture Library; p.46 (left) Werner Forman Archive, (right) Michael Holford; p.47 (upper and centre) MacQuitty Collection, (lower right) Werner Forman Archive; p.50 (left) C.M. Dixon, (right) Douglas Dickins; p.52 Douglas Dickins; p.53 (left) MacQuitty Collection, (upper and lower right) Robert Harding Picture Library; p.54 Michael Holford; p.55 (upper) Ann & Bury Peerless, (lower) Michael Holford; p.56 Ancient Art & Architecture Collection; p.57 (upper) C.M. Dixon, (lower) Ancient Art & Architecture Collection; p.58 Douglas Dickins; p.59 (left) Michael Holford, (upper, centre and lower right) C.M. Dixon; p.60 MacQuitty Collection; p.61 MacQuitty Collection; p.62 Sonia Halliday Photographs; p.63 (left) Doublas Dickins, (right) C.M. Dixon; p.64 (left and lower right) Ancient Art & Architecture Collection, (upper right) MacQuitty Collection; p.65 (upper) Ancient Art & Architecture Collection, (lower left and right) MacQuitty Collection; p.66 Werner Forman Archive; p.67 (left) Ancient Art & Architecture Collection, (right) Alan Hutchison Library; p.68 Werner Forman Archive; p.69 Sonia Halliday Photographs, p.70 Sonia Halliday Photographs; p.71 (upper and lower) Sonia Halliday Photographs.